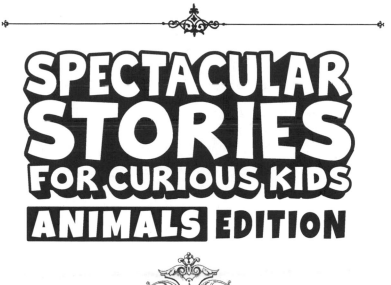

SPECTACULAR STORIES
FOR CURIOUS KIDS
ANIMALS EDITION

Contents

The Royal Goat Herd

Did you know that Great Britain has a herd of royal goats? The initial herd was started in 1837 when Mohommad Shah Qajar, who was the Shah of Persia, presented the goats as a gift to Queen Victoria when she became the queen. Some people might have gifted her jewelry or fancy trinkets, but a herd of goats sounds like a lot more fun!

The herd lived on Llandudno's Great Orme, an area of land in Wales with lots of good grazing. Here, the goat herd thrived. By 2001, the royal goat population had reached 250 and they were running out of the food that they ate! An estimated 85 goats were rehomed to different areas of Great Britain and the royal herd's lower numbers were again more manageable.

So what do they DO with these goats? Well, I think most of them just get to live a normal goat life, grazing and causing mischief. But a few of the goats get chosen for a very special mission.

In 2001, a goat who was a descendant of this royal goat bloodline was presented by Queen Elizabeth II to the First Battalion of the Royal Welsh, an infantry battalion of the British Army. This wasn't a new situation. The British monarchy has been presenting a goat to the Royal Welch Fusiliers from the royal herd since all the way back in 1844.

So what do they do with a goat? Well, the goat becomes an actual member of the British military. He is given an army number and everything. According to the BBC, he is "not a mascot, but a ranking member of the regiment."

The goat's name is William Windsor I, or Billy for short. His primary duty is to lead the battalion when they march in ceremonies or parades. Billy was assigned a handler who was officially called the "Goat Major." Billy held the title of lance corporal.

On June 16, 2006, Billy found himself in hot water. He traveled with his regiment to Cyprus, a small island in the Mediterranean in honor of Queen Elizabeth II's 80th birthday. Special guests to the parade included ambassadors from Sweden, the Netherlands, Argentina, and Spain, all very important people.

This was Billy's first time traveling overseas. Maybe it was nerves, but Billy began acting out. He became quite naughty, refused to march in line, and failed to keep step with the other soldiers. He even head-butted a drummer! Even his Goat Major could not keep him in line.

Billy was officially accused of the crimes of "unacceptable behavior", "lack of decorum", and "disobeying a direct order". He had to go in front of his commanding officer for a disciplinary hearing. That's kind of like a trial. Billy was demoted down to fusilier. The fusiliers had to salute him when he was a lance corporal, but not when he was their equal. This meant no more salutes and probably made him a sad goat. (Ok, probably not, but this is a fun story!)

In just three months, at the exact same place, Billy got the chance to redeem himself. It was time for the Alma Day parade. And there, Billy was able to regain his rank of lance corporal. His commanding officer said, "Billy performed exceptionally well, he has had all summer to reflect on his behavior at the Queen's birthday and clearly earned the rank he deserves."

In 2009, after 8 years of loyal service, Billy was retired. He was moved to live the easy life at Whipsnade Zoo where he is loved by children and zoo visitors.

To replace Billy, a trip to the royal goat herd was arranged. Thirty men from the 1st Battalion, as well as several veterinarians, were on hand to help select the next goat with big hooves to fill. A spokesman said, "We are looking for a goat which is calm under pressure and a team player."

It took some time, but they finally selected a 5-month-old goat. He will be named William of Windsor II and will begin training as a fusilier and have to work his way up the ranks. Let's hope he can keep his wits about him during parades and not head-butt any drummers!

These Rats Are Life Savers!

When you think of an animal that is trained to save lives, there might be several that come to mind. Perhaps a dog that is trained for search and rescue. Or maybe a miniature horse that acts as a therapy animal to help people struggling with illness. You probably don't think about a rat. But guess what! A group in Belgium is training rats that save lives.

Bart Weetjens likes to help people with problems. He heard that landmines were becoming dangerous in some areas of Africa. A landmine is an explosive device that is hidden below ground and will explode when people walk over top of them. Bad guys set landmines and lots of innocent people end up being hurt. Soldiers and police officers search for landmines, but detecting them can be really hard and dangerous.

Bart started to think outside of the box. He was a pet lover and wondered if animals could be trained to help. The work was still dangerous for dogs, as their size could trigger a landmine to explode. So he started to think about smaller animals. He remembered from his childhood that rats were very intelligent and social creatures. He put a team together and got to work.

The group, APOPO, started to train giant African pouch rats because they were so plentiful in the area. These rats have really good noses, meaning they can smell things that humans can't, like the explosives used in the landmines. Soldiers and police can have the rats explore a suspicious area first. If the rat smells the explosives, it will scratch the ground, alerting the people that it is dangerous. Then the humans can take the safe and proper steps to detonate the dangerous device. So what does the rat get if he is doing a good job? It turns out rats love special treats as their reward. Peanut butter and mushed-up banana is a favorite!

Rats started being used as helpers for detecting landmines in 2007. Since then, they have found over 56,000 landmines or other explosive devices. This means they have saved thousands of innocent lives. And not one rat has ever been hurt in the process.

With the success of landmine detection, APOPO started to think about other things that rats could use their good sniffers to help detect. Another problem in Africa is TB or tuberculosis. TB is a bacteria that causes people to get really sick and many people in Africa aren't vaccinated against it. Clinics that help to diagnose TB can become overwhelmed. Laboratory technicians have to work slowly and steadily to examine samples from sick people to see if they are actually sick with TB. But the rats can do it much faster! The rats can smell the samples and determine if it is contaminated with TB. If it is, they will alert their handler by keeping their nose near the sample and scratching at it.

Rats are much more efficient than humans. A job that takes a human laboratory technician all day can be done by a rat in only 7 minutes! Wow, these guys are fast.

Over the years, these hero rats, as APOPO calls them, have screened over 792,000 samples for TB and caught over 22,000 cases that were missed by lab technicians. And don't worry, the samples have been deactivated so that the rats and the handlers are all protected from getting TB.

So the next time someone says rats are gross, pesky critters, remember these special rats in Africa who are helping to save lives every day!

Why Did This Cat Wake Me Up?!

If you have a cat or know somebody with a cat, you may be aware that cats will occasionally wake you up in the middle of the night. Sometimes it's because they are playing, pouncing, and jumping like cats like to do. Sometimes it's because they are purring so loud that your bed seems to vibrate. But Mia Jansa's cat wakes her up for an extra special reason.

When Mia was young she was diagnosed with type one diabetes. This is when the pancreas doesn't make insulin. Insulin is needed to help the cells in the body regulate their blood sugar level. Without insulin, the body can have dangerous reactions. People with type one diabetes have to take quick finger stick blood tests many times throughout the day to make sure their blood sugar levels are where they're supposed to be.

Even at eight years old, Mia is a pro at checking her own blood sugar levels and is always sure to do it several times a day. If her levels seem out of balance, she and her parents can take the proper steps to keep her safe, such as taking insulin, eating, or drinking. But what about at night? The body can still get low blood sugar at night, but without frequent blood tests, a diabetic may not know it is happening. These are called hypoglycemic episodes and can result in a coma, dangerous medical conditions, or even death. In other words, this is serious stuff.

When Mia and her family adopted their cat, Pippa, Mia's diabetes wasn't on their mind. They loved Pippa because she had a beautiful black and white coat and a funny personality. They had no idea that Pippa would eventually offer the family such peace of mind when it came to Mia and her diabetes.

Not long after she had become part of the family, Pippa walked softly into Mia's room late one night and started meowing loudly. When she was awake, Mia rechecked her blood sugar. She discovered that the levels were frighteningly low. She woke up her mom, who helped her manage the situation and they were so grateful to Pippa for the wake-up call.

There have been several other times when Pippa has woken up Mia when her blood sugar levels were too low. If Mia won't wake up, she will sound the alarm for everyone in the house, meowing until one of Mia's parents checks on her. The whole family says that they rest easier knowing that Mia has a personal bodyguard keeping a watchful eye over her during the night.

What a sweet story of a rescue kitty who shows love to her family by keeping Mia safe!

A Man is Saved From a Mountain Lion by an Unlikely Hero

Robert Biggs spent a lot of time in the wilderness around his home in California. Many mornings he would head out for a hike and pan for gold in the nearby river. He enjoyed being in nature and observing all of the wildlife around him. He had no idea that his hike one spring morning would be so different from all of his other hikes!

Heading down a trail he had been down many times, he saw a mama bear and cubs sitting near a stream ahead of him. Robert was always careful to observe the creatures he saw, without threatening them or getting in their way. He hung back a distance and just watched the mama bear and cubs playing near the water.

After a little while, he decided it was time to move on. He turned to leave when something hit him hard from behind. The force knocked him to his knees. Something pulled his backpack up over his head. Robert was trapped! He saw that he was being attacked by a mountain lion.

The mountain lion had a hold of Robert's backpack, but it also bit Robert on the arm. Robert had a rock pick (a small ax used for breaking up rocks) with him, so he took a swing at the mountain lion with it. Before he could decide his next move he realized that a mama bear was joining the fight!

The bear grabbed the mountain lion by the neck and pulled it away from Robert. The two animals struggled on the ground before the mountain lion managed to escape. The mountain lion ran away quickly, not willing to take on an angry bear! The bear walked calmly back to her cubs.

Robert realized that the whole situation was really lucky. And he knows that the bear was likely not protecting him, but looking out for her cubs. Robert thinks that the mountain lion had been hiding and planning on preying on the cubs before he arrived. He thinks that he just got in the way of the mountain lion attacking the cubs. The mama bear knew her cubs were in danger and therefore wanted to get rid of the pesky mountain lion. Robert was sure glad that she showed up!

Luckily, Robert was not injured in the attack. He did have a few small wounds from the mountain lion's teeth, but he still continued his hike that day. He bandaged it up when he got home. Robert says he will still continue to hike in the woods, but his wife says she might be a little nervous!

Robert's story is a great reminder that animals in nature have their own rules and can sometimes be dangerous. It's always best to pay attention when you are out hiking or in an area with wild animals.

Unsinkable Sam

Cats are known for having nine lives. That's just our way of saying that cats are tough and hardy creatures. They don't really have nine lives. Or do they? A cat who became known as "Unsinkable Sam" might claim that he had at least three lives, as he survived three separate ships being attacked and sunk during a war.

A little black and white cat was loaded up and put on board the German battleship, the Bismarck. World War II was underway and the ocean was full of battleships, aircraft carriers, and other military boats. Often a crew would have several cats onboard known as ship's cats. These cats weren't for snuggling the sailors, although maybe they did that too. These fierce cats were hunters, making sure the rodent population on the ship was under control so they didn't damage important ropes, wires, documents, or furniture.

Little is known about this seagoing cat at this point. That's because a few months after he boarded the battleship it was attacked. Two thousand members of the crew died when the ship sank into the ocean. It was a terribly sad tragedy.

Later on that day, the British ship, HMS Cossack, was sailing through the wreckage when they saw a cat floating along on a piece of wood from the ship. Several of the crew members yelled, "Oscar, Oscar!" Oscar was an exclamation used by the International

Code of Signals to indicate "Man Overboard." The crew aboard the HMS Cossack managed to rescue the cat. They decided to keep him as their new ship's cat and gave him the appropriate name of Oscar.

Life was comfortable for Oscar during the nearly 6 months that he was aboard the HMS Cossack. But tragedy struck again when a German U-boat sent a torpedo straight into the ship. Huge fires began to spread and the boat was no longer drivable. Attempts to tow the boat to shore were unsuccessful. A massive explosion took out one-third of the ship. It was pure chaos on the ship as crews were trying to evacuate. No one was looking out for Oscar the cat. And yet they were all shocked to find that he had survived! Someone pulled him off the sinking boat and took him on a rescue boat to the shores of Gibraltar.

For most cats, this might have been the end of their days at sea, but not this guy. While he may not have had a choice, he was one fierce cat. Stories of his survival spread and he was renamed "Unsinkable Sam." Sam was transferred to live on the aircraft carrier the HMS Royal Ark. He would find that his time on the aircraft carrier would be short. About one month after his arrival, a torpedo hit the giant carrier, causing it to take on massive amounts of water. Again, attempts to tow it to shore proved to be worthless and crews needed to be rescued. Sam was reportedly picked up out of the water where he was clinging to a floating plank. He was said to be "angry but quite unharmed."

Again, Sam and the crew made it safely back to shore. That was to be Sam's last journey as a ship's cat. He was transferred to live at the office of the Governor of Gibraltar. Later he was sent up to live in Belfast at the "Home for Sailors." I'm sure Sam and the sailors had a good time sharing the memories of their days spent exploring the seas. I doubt many other sailors could boast that they survived three separate ships sinking! Sam died of old age when he was 14 years old.

The Oldest Animal in the World

Do you ever feel like your parents are, well...OLD?!? What about your grandparents? They've probably been around a while and witnessed a lot of history. But even if you have great-grandparents, they haven't been around as long as one particular turtle. That's because Jonathan the Tortoise is 190 years old!

Yep, he's a pretty old dude! Jonathan is the oldest animal (technically a reptile) alive. Vets and researchers aren't quite sure when he was born and think he could be even older than that. He was originally living in the Seychelle Archipelago but was brought to St. Helena Island in the southern Atlantic, in 1882. Here he was given as a gift to Sir William Grey-Wilson. A few years later, Sir William became the governor of St. Helena Island, so Jonathan got to move to the governor's residence, known as the Plantation House.

Somewhere along the way, it was decided that Jonathan would continue to stay at Plantation House. This is where he still lives today. As I write this, Jonathan is still wandering around the gardens of the Plantation, greeting the guests and tourists who come to see him. Jonathan is blind and has lost his sense of smell, but he doesn't let that stop him from enjoying himself. His time is spent grazing, sunbathing, sleeping, and of course, eating. What are his favorite foods? Bananas, carrots, cabbage, and apples are a few of his favorite snacks. He lives with three tortoise friends, Emma, Fred, and David.

190 years is a long time and Jonathan has been around to see a lot of history take place. Let's think about a few things this tortoise has been alive for. Thirty-one governors have lived in the Plantation House while Jonathan has lived there. He has been alive for 40 United States Presidents. He has seen the beginning and end of two World Wars. From ships to cars, airplanes, and even rockets, Jonathan's life has spanned many years of world exploration. What a cool thing to think of all of the stories this guy could tell... if only tortoises could talk!

So how old do tortoises usually live? Many tortoises have a lifespan of 80-150 years. Jonathan has probably been able to survive for such a long time because he is well-fed and doesn't have to be concerned about predators. The oldest recorded tortoise was Adwaita, a tortoise living in a zoo in India who died in 2006. Some of her caretakers suspected she was 250 years old!

Tortoises aren't known for having great speed. In fact, their average walking speed is only about a quarter of a mile per hour. Not very fast! But I guess with life, it's kind of like the story of the tortoise and the hare. Slow and steady wins the race!

First Chimp in Space

When the United States Air Force was researching how to launch a man into outer space, they didn't start with a man. They actually launched a chimpanzee into space first to make sure that the necessary tasks for flying a spaceship could still be performed while in space.

Ham the chimp was born in Cameroon in 1957. Two years later he was purchased by the United States Air Force. His adventure was just beginning.

Ham was part of a group of forty space chimpanzees at Holloman Air Force Base. These chimps were all in training to perform a few of the necessary tasks for flying a spaceship. The chimps were trained and evaluated to see which one would be the best candidate. For training, the chimps were taught to respond to electronic lights and sound. They learned to push a lever within five seconds of seeing a flashing blue light. If the chimp performed correctly, he received a banana pellet.

The group of chimps capable of performing the tasks correctly got smaller and smaller until there were only 6 chimps remaining. On January 31, 1961, Ham made history. He was the chimp chosen to launch into space from Cape Canaveral, Florida. On that day, Ham was treated just as any astronaut would be treated. He had a custom space suit and was outfitted in a special seat that was just his size. On the morning of the launch, he rode in the same van that would take astronauts to their shuttles. Even the Mercury capsule he rode in was identical to the ones that would launch future astronauts.

At this time, Ham was only being called No. 65. That is because the officials involved in the space launch didn't want a bunch of bad press if he didn't survive the launch. They figured that if he had a cute name, people would be more worried and protest using chimpanzees for their research. Luckily, Ham's story has a happy ending.

When Ham was launched into his sub-orbital flight, ground crews were able to monitor his vital signs. His special space suit kept him safe, even when his capsule experienced a brief loss of pressure. Ham was able to push his lever, just as he had been taught during training. His reaction time was only half a second slower than his times had been on earth, proving that these tasks could be performed easily in space.

As was planned, Ham's spacecraft crashed back to the earth and landed in the Atlantic Ocean. Ham was rescued shortly after by the USS Donner that was waiting nearby. He had a small bruise on his nose from the crash, but other than that he was just fine. He was the first chimp to fly in space! His flight lasted 16 minutes and 39 seconds.

After a safe landing, the crew decided this chimpanzee needed a name. They settled on the name Ham, as an acronym for the place where he was trained, the Holloman Aerospace Medical Center. He was eventually taken to the National Zoo in Washington

D.C. where he lived for 17 years. He was later relocated to the North Carolina Zoo to live with a small group of chimps. He lived to be 26 years old. Ham was buried at the International Space Hall of Fame Museum in New Mexico. It was only fitting to include him as one of the many who helped make space exploration possible.

As a direct result of Ham's space mission, the United States felt confident in sending one of its citizens into outer space. Not even six months later, Alan Shepherd became the first American to fly in space. That happened because a chimpanzee had shown scientists and researchers that it was possible!

The Escaped Pig That Almost Caused a War

In the 1800s, the relationship between Great Britain and the United States was often a bit strained. Borders between lands needed to be very specific to prevent any further discontent amongst the citizens. A treaty signed in 1846 between the two countries clarified the border between the United States and Canada. Unfortunately, nothing specific was mentioned about the San Juan Islands, just off the coast that bordered both countries.

With good fishing and soil, citizens of both countries settled on the islands. Things seemed mostly peaceful, but a pig was about to change all of that and rewrite history!

On June 15, 1859, American farmer, Lyman Cutler went out to his garden to find a pig eating his potatoes. This was not the first time his garden had been uprooted by a roaming pig and Lyman was understandably annoyed. He may have acted a bit rash though, as he decided to shoot and kill the pig.

The pig was owned by British farmer, Charles Griffon. Charles was not too happy to hear that his pig had been shot and killed. He was even less happy when Lyman offered to pay him only $10 for the incident.

Charles demanded that he should receive at least $100 as payment for his deceased pig.

Lyman said to Charles, "It was eating my potatoes!" Charles replied, "It is up to you to keep your potatoes out of my pig!"

Oh boy! Things escalated from there. Charles reached out to the British authorities who threatened to arrest Lyman. Other American citizens became outraged at this prospect, so they called the American military for protection.

The Americans sent 67 American soldiers to keep watch and protect the American citizens from British rule. In response, the British sent three warships to land just outside the island. Things were getting serious!

Tension continued to rise as each military group expanded. Before too long the American side totaled 461 soldiers with 14 cannons. The British had five warships at the ready with 70 guns and 2,140 men. War was looming.

When the British governor of the island demanded that the British troops dislodge the American troops, the British commanders refused. They said that they would not start a war between two great nations "over a squabble about a pig."

Word got back to the leaders in Washington D.C. and London, and both governments were shocked that things had gotten to that level. They worked quickly to diffuse the situation and come up with a peaceful negotiation. Both sides agreed to withdraw the bulk of their troops. Affairs were calm for the next ten years as both countries worked through negotiations. The United States eventually gained control of the San Juan Islands, but it was done without any war.

Nothing else is known about the pesky potato-eating pig that started the whole conflict. But I guess it's a good lesson to keep your pigs out of your neighbor's garden!

Stop Monkeying Around!

The year was 1935. Frank Buck's Jungle Camp was a popular tourist destination. Located on Long Island, New York, the forty-acre "camp" was the home to lions, tigers, elephants, and other wild animals. But the main attraction was Monkey Mountain, a 75-foot tall man-made mountain that was the home of 570 rhesus monkeys.

The story of Frank Buck's Jungle Camp is a fascinating tale. Frank was born in Texas, but he was a rambler and worked his way north to Chicago. He won $3500 in a poker game, a fairly tidy sum back in those days and Frank decided to treat himself to his first trip to another country. He traveled to Brazil where he managed to capture quite a few live exotic birds. Frank brought the birds back to the United States, where he was amazed at how much money he could make selling them to wealthy people. An exotic animal collector was born.

Frank became well versed in foreign travel and capturing wild animals. He traveled with the animals on the steamships to make sure they stayed safe on the journey back to America where he sold them to zoos and private buyers. In 1933, Frank set up a display at the Chicago World Fair with an assortment of animals from his travels. His exhibition was a success and when the fair closed, Frank moved all of the animals to what became known as Frank Buck's Jungle Camp in New York.

Newspapers often reported on the animals at the park, noting any new arrivals from abroad and publishing any births of baby animals. But in 1935, Frank's park received some different type of press, when the monkeys made a break for it!

Slightly before lunchtime on a fall day, one of the zookeepers entered Monkey Mountain armed with his cleaning supplies. He lowered a board across the moat around the monkey enclosure and balanced his way across the board to reach the other side. Then he set to work cleaning and scrubbing.

For a few minutes, the zookeeper was so immersed in his job that he didn't notice what was happening. But then he looked up and saw it! Monkeys were scurrying across the moat on the makeshift bridge at an alarming rate. The zookeeper hurried into action, alerting the ticket seller and other employees about the escaped monkeys. With visitors to the zoo watching in alarm, all the workers scrambled about but were only able to recapture two of the little monkeys before they disappeared into the woods and beyond to wreak havoc on the rest of Long Island.

It is reported that the rest of the zoo animals went into hysterics at the sight of the monkeys on the loose, with the lions and tigers roaring. An estimated 175 monkeys were now on the loose somewhere on Long Island!

A few hours later, police had managed to capture only two of the little escapees. The 4 pm train heading east had to come to an abrupt halt as it surged along the tracks. Fifty of the monkeys were on the tracks, hooting, chattering, and having a wild time. The train conductor, who had read of such things in other countries, was able to clear the tracks with just a five-minute train delay.

With nightfall rapidly approaching, thirty of the little guys decided they'd had enough fun and returned to Monkey Mountain, but this still left plenty of monkeys on the loose. Zoo workers and police notified the public of the problem. They were concerned that unprepared citizens might wake up in the morning to find a monkey in or on top of their houses. Looking to make the story more spectacular, the zoo workers said that the monkey escape was due to the plotting of one monkey in particular, the ringleader named Capone.

The public took to the effort of trying to recapture the escaped primates, especially as they were promised cash rewards or a free annual pass to the zoo. While many of the monkeys were returned to the zoo, reports fail to mention if ALL of the monkeys were ever recaptured. One can only hope that at least a few of those escaped monkeys managed to claim their freedom and live it up somewhere on the island!

The Incredible Story of Elsa

Usually, when people think of lions, they think of the King of the Jungle, a big fierce beast that roars and eats everything. While it's true that lions can be fierce, tenacious hunters, in this story you will learn about a lion who enjoyed humans...as friends!

This is the story of Elsa the Lioness. If you have ever thought it would be cool to have a lion living in your backyard, then this is the story for you.

George and Joy Adamson had a lot of respect for the African wilderness where they lived. Joy was an artist, studying and painting the customs of African tribes. George was a game warden, trying to keep people and animals safe on the Kenya plains. They both spent their days enjoying the beauty of the nature and wildlife surrounding them.

In 1956, George was out patrolling when he was aggressively attacked by a lion. Unfortunately, he was forced to kill the lion who attacked him in order to survive. It was only later that he realized that the lion who attacked him was a mother protecting her three cubs. George rescued the three cubs and brought them to his house.

His wife, Joy, was adamant that they had to feed and care for these lion cub sisters. They named the cubs Big One, Lustica, and Elsa. They were only four days old. The cubs were bottle-fed a mixture of unsweetened milk, cod oil, and bone meal. They were allowed to roam the property during the day. At night, they were locked in a secured enclosure to protect them from other lions, hyenas, and jackals, all of whom might be hunting for a tasty snack. They were treated almost like you would treat a pet, but these were definitely no ordinary house pets!

George and Joy fed and cared for the cubs for months. But later in the year, the Kenya Game Department decided that the Adamsons could only keep one of the lion cubs. The other two would need a new home. It was decided that Big One and Lustica had the best chance of thriving out in the world. They were bigger and stronger than Elsa. The Kenya Game Department decided that Big One and Lustica would be transferred to the Rotterdam Zoo in the Netherlands. Elsa would remain in Kenya.

Big One and Lustica would have to travel by airplane to get to their new home. George and Joy worried about this transition. They tried to prepare the cubs the best they could by taking them on daily drives in their truck. They hoped this would help them get used to traveling. When the time came to transfer the two lions, Joy and George went with them to the airport. It was a 180-mile drive, so Elsa would stay at home. Joy said that when they were loaded in the truck and driving down the driveway, Elsa ran along beside with the saddest look on her face. A new adventure awaited her now.

With Lustica and Big One gone, Joy decided that the best thing to do for Elsa was to train her so that she could survive in the wild. She knew that Elsa would be happiest, living her life as a wild lion, the way she was supposed to do. The Adamsons worked together for several months, teaching Elsa how to be a wild cat and survive in the wilderness. They taught her how to hunt and how to live on her own.

When she was old enough and big and strong enough, the Adamsons said goodbye to their friend and released her into the wild. It would be a while before they saw her again and they would hope that they had made the right choice. When she was three years old, Elsa returned to the Adamsons, this time with three of her own cubs with her. The Adamsons would name the cubs Jespah, Gopa, and Little Elsa.

For a while, the Adamsons enjoyed seeing the cubs and Elsa on occasion while Elsa was raising her little ones. But unfortunately, two years later, Elsa died of babesiosis, a tick-born illness common in cats in Africa. Her grave is in Meru National Park.

Without their mother's friendly demeanor toward the Adamsons to guide them, the cubs began to pull away from George and Joy. They kept their distance. Eventually, they began to cause problems for local farmers by killing livestock and Joy was worried about their safety. It was decided that the cubs needed to be captured and released somewhere else.

It took a while but the cubs, who were young lions by this point, were eventually captured and released onto the Serengeti, a massive amount of protected land in eastern Africa that is the home to many species of animals.

Despite spending a lot of time searching for them, Elsa's offspring seemed to vanish after they were released. Joy and George hoped this meant they were doing well. The only sighting was of Little Elsa, who was seen only once by George. She was with two unrelated lions when he saw her.

The story of Elsa brought worldwide attention to animal conservation, especially lions. Joy and George both wrote books on their adventures with the lions and the way they changed their lives. The movie *Born Free* was adapted from one of Joy's books and it received many awards and accolades. Even though the Adamsons have both died, their legacy continues through organizations aimed at protecting wildlife. Elsa's story is an exceptional tale of the beauty of humans and animals living together.

Prisoner of War

Judy had a heart for adventure right from the start. Born at a breeding kennel in Shanghai, China, the purebred English Pointer puppy somehow escaped when she was only three months old. She was found by a shopkeeper and received care for 6 months before a kennel worker spotted her and returned her to the breeding kennel. Originally called Shudi, the name was later changed to Judy.

About the same time that Judy was returned to her original home, a crew of the British Royal Navy decided they needed a mascot. Several other crews of ships all had mascots, so the sailors aboard the HMS Gnat decided they should have a mascot, as well. This would prove to be a good and life-saving decision for the crew!

The captain of the boat purchased Judy and presented her to the crew. His original intent was to have her trained to help with hunting birds, but within days it became clear that the crew was treating her as more of a pet and less of a working dog. The captain stated that she would only point as a trained pointer if there was food in the area. Luckily, Judy would still prove her worth with her affection. She also was known for alerting the crew with her barking if there were pirates or other thieves in the area.

Judy was given a box and a blanket to sleep on and trained to stay out of certain areas on the boat. She fell overboard one time and the crew immediately halted the ship and deployed a lifeboat to rescue Judy. In the ship's log, the event was recorded as a man overboard exercise. Another adventure happened when the HMS Gnat met up with the USS Panay for a party for the two crews. Upon leaving, the crew realized they didn't have Judy. They radioed to the crew of the USS Panay but they responded that they didn't have Judy either. Word got around that the USS Panay did indeed have Judy on their ship. A few members of the crew from HMS Gnat snuck aboard the USS Panay and stole the ship's bell leaving behind a ransom note for the return of Judy. Within an hour, Judy was safely back with her crew on the HMS Gnat.

World War II would find many members of the HMS Gnat transferred to the HMS Grasshopper and eventually deployed to a base in Singapore. Judy was included in this transfer. Judy was valuable to the crew on this ship as she was able to hear incoming aircraft before any of the crew members and would alert them to take cover.

One day in 1942, the HMS Grasshopper was hit with 2 bombs, causing the ship to begin to sink. Crews evacuated the ship and rowed to a nearby island. It was only upon arriving on the island that they realized Judy was not with them. A crewman went back, to check on Judy and get any supplies that might be available. Luckily, Judy was just fine! She made it to the island

and immediately began searching for fresh water. The island was uninhabited and had no food or apparent drinking water. Judy saved the day again! She began to dig around and located a freshwater drinking spring for herself and all the men.

Eventually, a boat rescued the crew and Judy and took them to another location. From here, they had to travel 200 miles to reach their destination and ride home. Along the way, Judy was attacked by a crocodile and got a big cut on her shoulder. Luckily, they patched her up with a first aid kit and she survived. Unfortunately, by the time the men arrived at their destination, the Japanese had taken over and they were taken as prisoners of war.

Judy was the only animal to be officially registered as a prisoner of war. Sometimes the prison guards knew about her. Other times, the crewmen had to hide her to keep her safe. They saved tiny bits of their rations to feed her, and she could also sneak out of the camp and kill rats and snakes for food. Many times the guards threatened to kill Judy, but her crew always kept her safe.

In 1944, Judy and the crew were transferred to Singapore. Dogs were not allowed on the boat, but one of the men, Frank Williams, who was particularly fond of Judy, trained her to be carried in a rice bag. He carried her onboard, over his shoulder, and stood on the deck with her for three hours. She was still and silent as if she knew not to get caught. There were more than 700 prisoners aboard the crowded ship.

During the night a torpedo hit the ship carrying Judy and all the prisoners. As the ship began to sink, Frank pushed Judy out of a porthole to give her the best chance of survival. Over 500 prisoners wouldn't survive the ship sinking, but those that did told of a dog who helped them by bringing them floating debris to help them stay afloat.

Frank gave up hope of seeing Judy again, but they were reunited four weeks later at another prisoner camp. Judy, Frank, and the other prisoners worked together to stay safe. The men looked out for Judy, just as she looked out for them. Finally, hope arrived in the form of allied troops in 1945.

The remaining prisoners had a safe ride back to England, but once again Judy was not supposed to be allowed onboard! Do you think that stopped them? Of course not! They snuck Judy onto the ship, where the cook kept her safe, hidden, and well-fed. Only three days before the ship's arrival in England did Frank tell the captain about the stowaway.

Judy had to quarantine for six months with Frank and other crew members visiting her regularly. The story of her heroics during the war spread and she was awarded several important awards. Judy and Frank were interviewed by a television crew and her barks were broadcast around the world. In her later years, Judy and Frank would visit the families of other soldiers who hadn't made it home. Frank said that Judy always seemed to offer feelings of peace and comfort to the family members.

Judy passed away when she was 14 years old. Frank spent two months building a granite and marble memorial with a plaque that told the dog's story. She was truly a hero to so many people and led an incredible and adventurous life!

Mike the Headless Chicken

One fine morning in 1945, Lloyd Olsen set out to his yard to catch and prepare a chicken for that night's dinner. His wife, Clara, had invited her mother over for dinner that evening and wanted to prepare a tasty meal of fried chicken. During the 1940s, raising and preparing your own chicken was fairly common, especially in the small town of Fruita, Colorado. But as it turns out, there was nothing fairly common about the chicken that Lloyd set about to kill that morning.

Upon selecting the chicken and lowering the ax to cut off the chicken's head, a strange thing happened. Somehow, although most of the chicken's head was cut off, the ax failed to cut the jugular vein or the brain stem. This chicken was still very much alive, even though it didn't have a head!

Lloyd was aghast at this new situation, as he had never seen or heard of anything like it. He decided that if this chicken had the will to live, he'd help it along. The chicken was named Mike, although no one is sure if that name came along before or after the beheading. Lloyd fed Mike a mixture of water and chicken meal from an eyedropper. He claims that Mike could still peck for food, sit on a perch and walk around, although rather clumsily.

A week after Mike's miraculous survival, Lloyd and Clara decided to hit the road with their chicken.

First, they headed to the University of Utah where amazed scientists did some studying of the bird. It seemed that with his brain stem still intact, he was able to receive all the normal chicken reflex messages and live a normal life.

But from here Mike's life was anything but ordinary because he became a pretty famous guy. Lloyd hired a manager for Mike and the chicken and his entourage started touring the country. Mike was able to land spots in side shows in New York City, Atlantic City, Los Angeles, and San Diego where people were paying $0.25 for a chance to see a headless chicken. For a few months, Lloyd and Clara were earning $4500 a month (about $55,000 today)! This was all thanks to Mike. Because of his value, Mike was insured for $10,000, which was about $120,000 in today's dollars.

Mike received a ton of publicity and was often photographed for magazines and newspaper articles. The famous chicken was even featured in *Time* and *Life* magazines!

Eighteen months after he nearly died for the first time, Mike's luck ran out. He was eating a piece of corn in a motel in Arizona when he began to choke and died.

But the country still celebrates Mike the headless chicken, especially the town of Fruita, Colorado, where Mike is still quite famous. Every year, Fruita holds an annual Mike the Headless Chicken Festival. Visitors to the festival can participate in a 5K Run Like A Headless Chicken Race, play a game of egg toss, or Pin the Head on the Chicken. I think this gives a whole new meaning to running around like a chicken with your head cut off!

Lions Save the Life of a
12-Year-Old Girl

Have you ever wanted a superhero to run in at the last second and save the day for you? Maybe you're getting picked on by a sibling or just having a bad day. Well, a girl in Ethiopia did have some superheroes swoop in at the last second. These superheroes were a pride of lions and they saved her life!

A twelve-year-old girl living in Ethiopia was walking home from school one day when she was kidnapped by some bad men. The bad guys took her to a remote area where they had her captured. I'm sure the poor girl thought she'd never see her family again.

Police were working really hard to find her, but it was taking them time to narrow down the search. Then, a pride of lions came across the little girl. A pride is a group of lions, a pack. And what happened next was simply incredible.

The lions not only chased away the girl's kidnappers, but they stayed with her and guarded her until the police were able to get there. When the police arrived, the lions just walked away. That's a pretty impressive group of bodyguards this lucky girl had!

Some people think this story is suspicious and that maybe the lions were planning on eating the girl. But one wildlife expert has an explanation. He suspects that, because the girl was crying, the lions knew that she was an innocent cub and their instincts were to protect her.

Animals can sense if people are feeling fearful or nervous. Some animals can even read us by how fast our hearts are beating. These hero lions knew that this girl was a cub and even better, they somehow knew that her kidnappers were bad men. They could sense that the police were there to help the girl instead of hurt her.

The amazed police reunited her with her family. They could hardly believe it and they were there to see it! This story turned out to have a happy ending, all thanks to a pride of awesome superhero lions. This should probably be made into a TV show. I know I'd watch a show about a lion pride that went around saving kids in trouble!

Presidential Pets

If you were moving into the White House, you'd certainly want to bring your pets with you, right? Many of the presidents who have lived in the White House felt the same way. Because of this, the White House has been the home to a number of presidential pets. What's the most popular pet among past presidents? The dog comes in as number one, with 30 of the past 45 presidents having at least one dog in the White House. There have been quite a few cats and even some birds and guinea pigs.

There have also been some crazy animals living in the White House. Let's learn about a few of the unconventional pets that called it home.

In 1825, President John Quincy Adams hosted French Revolution War hero, Marquis de Lafayette at the White House. Lafayette brought a gift for John Adams...an alligator! In those days, exotic animals were thought of as extravagant gifts. The president decided that the alligator could live in the East Room, a room in the White House that was still being finished, but it did have its own bathtub. It was the perfect place to house an alligator. According to rumors, President Adams used to scare unsuspecting visitors by giving them a tour of the White House, complete with a stop to visit the East Room and its scaly reptile!

President Martin Van Buren was also the recipient of an unusual gift during his presidency. The Sultan of Oman gave him two baby tiger cubs! President Van Buren wanted to keep them and let them grow up in the White House. However, Congress argued that the tiger cubs had actually been given to the United States, not President Van Buren personally. Congress ended up winning the debate and the cubs were sent to live at a zoo in Washington. This was probably for the best. Can you imagine two tigers roaming the halls of the White House?

Luckily, when Calvin Coolidge came along, Congress decided to let him keep his animal gift. In 1926, farmers from different states were all trying to win the honor of providing food for the Presidential Thanksgiving meal. Someone from Mississippi sent a raccoon to be eaten! President Coolidge had never eaten a raccoon, and he wasn't eager to try. Instead, he and his wife decided to keep the raccoon as a pet. They named her Rebecca and she lived a fancy life! She was well fed, with shrimp, persimmons, and eggs being her favorites. For Christmas, she received a collar embroidered with *White House Racoon*. She was allowed to roam free in the house and the First Lady even had a tree house built just for her. Rebecca was a mischief-maker, and many of the workers weren't as fond of her. She was known for unscrewing light bulbs, opening cabinets, and uprooting houseplants. What a prankster!

Other animals weren't allowed inside the White House, but they did live and graze in the surrounding fenced yard. Woodrow Wilson wanted to lower the cost of lawn cutting during World War I. He bought a flock of sheep and turned them out in the yard to keep the grass trimmed. At the beginning of White House history, nearly every president had at least one horse or pony that resided in the White House stables. As automobiles became more popular, not as many presidents felt the need to have a horse. Not John F. Kennedy though. He had several ponies for his children that roamed freely on the property. Macaroni, probably the most photographed of his ponies, was owned by his daughter, Caroline. President Kennedy was the last president to have horses at the White House.

It's nice to know that if you ever move into the White House, you could take your animals with you. Unless you have a tiger. Congress does frown on that one. What exotic animal would you want to get as a gift if you were the president?

Pickles the Soccer Dog

In 1966, England was all set to host the FIFA World Cup. The best soccer (or football as they say in England) players in the world would compete for their countries with a chance to earn the title of champion, as well as the coveted Jules Rimet Trophy. With the World Cup beginning in July, the trophy was usually kept at the Football Association headquarters but during March, it was on display as an exhibition.

The trophy was insured for about $30,000 (even though it was really only valued at $3,000) so it was guarded around the clock. The only time guards weren't present was during a Sunday morning church service near the exhibition hall.

So you can imagine the shock when guards arrived at noon on Sunday to find that the trophy was missing! Someone had taken the door to the exhibition hall off its hinges. They had removed the padlock keeping the trophy in its case, and the trophy...was GONE!

Police set to work interviewing people and trying to get a lead on who had stolen the trophy. The next day the chairman of the Football Association, Joe Mears, received a phone call. It was an anonymous caller stating that Joe would be receiving a package. Sure enough, the next day a package arrived. It contained a removable lining from the top of the trophy and a ransom note demanding $15,000 for its return. The note said that if the instructions weren't properly followed, the trophy would be melted.

Despite being told to keep the police out of it, Joe Mears knew his best chance of retrieving the trophy would involve the police. They helped him navigate this tricky situation. They made a bag full of fake money, only putting the real money directly at the top.

When it came time to make the switch, police were able to arrest the thief. But it turned out that he didn't have the trophy after all. He claimed he was only acting as a middleman, being the one to collect the ransom, and didn't know where the actual trophy was.

At this point, you are probably wondering if this story even has anything to do with animals. We are getting there!

A few days after the trail had gone cold with the case of the missing trophy, David Corbett was taking his dog, Pickles, for a walk. Pickles was a black and white border collie. Pickles pulled David over to a hedge near their property and began to sniff excitedly. David saw a package wrapped tightly in a newspaper. When he unwrapped it, David was astonished by what he saw. He recognized the missing Jules Rimet Trophy right away!

David notified the police who arrived to take the trophy. At first, they thought David might be a suspect, but luckily, he had an alibi. That meant that he could prove that he was somewhere else when the trophy was stolen.

Pickles wasn't a trained police dog, but he sure was a hero! He became a brief celebrity and even appeared in some TV shows and movies. His owner, David, got to attend the player's celebration dinner when England finally won the World Cup later that summer. David and Pickles received reward money of about $6,000. David used it to buy a house where he and Pickles lived until Pickles died in 1967. He was buried in the backyard.

Pickles' story is an example that you don't have to have fancy training to help do the right thing!

War Time Pig

During World War 2, the United States government began selling war bonds to help fund all of the things needed to help with the war. War bonds were purchased by 84 million Americans and were thought to be patriotic, and a way for Americans to help to do their part to support the war.

An unlikely hero was born in 1942. Part of a litter of 12, a pig, who later became known as King Neptune, was raised on a small family farm in southern Illinois. He was raised as a 4-H project by the farmer's daughter and was donated to be served at a fundraising dinner when a Navy officer decided he had bigger plans for the pig.

Don C. Lingle thought he had some potential to auction off the pig in order to sell war bonds. The war bonds would be used to fund the battleship, *Illinois*, which was already under construction. Don set out with an auctioneer and they traveled all around southern Illinois, auctioning off the pig. At the close of each auction, the pig was always returned so he could be auctioned off again the next night.

King Neptune, as he was named, was a Hereford swine, meaning he was mostly red with a white face and legs. Don would dress the pig in a blue Navy blanket and adorn him with a crown and earrings. The people loved it! King Neptune auctions were in high demand and eventually, Don decided to auction off the individual parts of the pig to raise even more money. King Neptune was never harmed and he helped bring in so much money. The pig's squeal was sold for $25 on at least one occasion. One of his bristle hairs sold for $500. And in 1943, the Illinois governor purchased King Neptune for the state of Illinois for $1 million dollars!

By the time the war was over, King Neptune had raised over $19 million dollars in war bonds to help with the war effort. This was some pig!

With the war over, Don heard that King Neptune was supposed to be heading for the Chicago Stockyards where he would likely become bacon. Don wasn't going to allow that to happen so he managed to gain ownership of the pig. He sent him to live out the rest of his life as a happy pig at a small farm in southern Illinois. When he passed away, he was buried with military honors and the state of Illinois built a memorial to honor him, the pig who helped raise so much money for the war.

The Bird That Saved 194 Lives

A pigeon is an unlikely war hero. When I think about courageous war animals, I usually think about brave war horses and daring military dogs. But in this story, the hero who saved the day came in the form of a carrier pigeon, who rescued 194 men. This pigeon did it all, while wounded in action.

During World War I, the military had 600 carrier pigeons that could be used to assist in sending messages. While the birds were not quite as reliable as radio or telegraphs, they had the benefit of being harder for the enemy to intercept. The birds could fly up to 50 miles per hour carrying their messages in tiny leg canisters, backpacks, or chest packs. Small, but fast, these birds made difficult targets for the enemy to shoot down.

In 1918, 554 men from the United States Army's 77th Infantry division became trapped in a ravine in northern France surrounded by German soldiers. While they were hidden from the German soldiers, because they were so close to the enemy, the men were being accidentally hit with ammo from their own side. With food and ammunition supplies running low, the commander of the unit had no choice but to get creative with sending messages.

Major Whittlesey prepared his first message, "*Many wounded. We cannot evacuate.*" He sent up the first carrier pigeon to deliver the message.

Then he watched as it was shot out of the sky by a German sniper.

He tried again with a second message, "*Men are suffering. Can support be sent?*" Unfortunately, this one suffered the same fate as the first bird.

By now Major Whittlesey had only one bird left. This bird's name was Cher Ami. That translates from French as "dear friend." Cher Ami was a Black Check pigeon who had been raised and trained in Great Britain. He had served the troops well so far in this war and was a trusted carrier. He was also their last hope.

The final message was placed in the pigeon's leg canister. It read, "*We are along the road parallel to 276.4. Our own artillery is dropping a barrage directly on us. For heaven's sake, stop it.*"

The brave Cher Ami flew into the air. He was almost immediately hit with shrapnel that severed his right leg and left a cut on his chest. The pigeon fell to the ground.

I would imagine the soldiers in that ravine were feeling pretty defeated at this point. But imagine their surprise when they noticed the little bird rising up again, defying the odds and lifting into the air. This time, the bird would make it, delivering the message to the command post 25 miles away.

Upon arrival, Cher Ami was evaluated and found to have lost an eye, as well as a leg. He was sent into immediate emergency surgery where he survived and recovered. His mission was a success, as the friendly fire was immediately halted and 194 men were rescued and managed to safely make it back to the American side.

Cher Ami received an award from France, the Croix de Guerre, for his military heroics. He also was given a small wooden leg that had been fashioned by some of the men that he had helped to save. The bird was then sent back home to New Jersey to live out his days in a place much quieter than a military battlefield.

When Cher Ami died, his body was donated to the famous Smithsonian museum in Washington D.C. A taxidermist was hired to prepare the bird who is now on display at the museum as a brave and surprising war hero.

An Unlikely Champion

The first Saturday in May is a big deal to horse racing fans all over the world. Perhaps you've heard of the Kentucky Derby, the fastest two minutes in sports?

The Kentucky Derby has been raced since 1875. The top three-year-old Thoroughbred horses all gather at Churchill Downs in Louisville, Kentucky to see who will win the blanket of roses, a huge cash prize, and the coveted title of Derby Champion.

The majority of these top racehorses have been Derby contenders since the moment they were born, the result of careful breeding and raising. Early training with the very best riders and outstanding care helps these horses be the best they can be. Without a doubt, they deserve to be racing in this prestigious race.

But every once in a while a horse comes out of nowhere and steals the spotlight. And that's exactly what happened in the running of the 2022 Kentucky Derby when Rich Strike bested the entire field of horses and claimed the championship for himself. Everyone loves it when an underdog, a competitor whom most think has no chance of winning, shows up and rewrites history.

Rich Strike was born on a farm in Kentucky. He started his training as a two-year-old but didn't seem to be very fast. His owners weren't super impressed with him and decided to sell him in a claiming race for $30,000. This may seem like a lot of money, but many racehorses sell for hundreds of thousands and even millions, so Rich Strike was a pretty cheap deal.

The new owner, Richard Dawson, was fairly new to horse racing. He was becoming a little discouraged with the business and was considering getting out of it. But he loved the horses and the excitement so he decided to give it one more shot. He met trainer Eric Reed and decided to buy Rich Strike. Eric saw something special in the horse that no one else did.

As a three-year-old, Rich Strike was entered in several races in the spring. He finished third, fourth, and third. Not bad, but not great either.

In order to qualify for the Derby, race horses need to earn points from their placings in previous races. The twenty horses with the most points are eligible to run in the Derby. Rich Strike didn't make the cut. He sat in 21st place with his number of points. Another horse would have to scratch or pull out of the race in order for Rich Strike to have a shot at running in the Derby.

At 8:45 on Friday morning before the famous race, Rich Strike's trainer was told no horses had scratched the race so Rich Strike wouldn't be allowed to run. However, at the last second, just minutes before the officials were going to close the race and finalize the horses, the trainer got the phone call he had been hoping for, "Do you want to run Rich Strike in the Derby?" A last-second scratch from another horse had opened up a spot for Rich Strike. He was going to run in the Derby!

The lineup of horses for the 2022 Kentucky Derby was incredibly talented. Several of these horses had won big prestigious races and lots of money. Rich Strike had never even won a race! His trainer had never had a horse compete in the Derby. His jockey was young and had never ridden in the Derby and never even won a big race. Needless to say, most people didn't expect too much from Rich Strike. In racing, officials use odds to determine the likelihood people think a horse will win a race. Rich Strike's odds were 80-1, some of the worst in Derby history! People didn't think he had a chance.

When the gates opened for the running of the Kentucky Derby, Rich Strike settled into 18th place. During the course of the mile and a quarter race, he would begin to gain on the leaders, passing tired horses easily. In the final stretch, he managed to pass the first place horse and he would go under the finish line as the clear winner! I can only imagine how loud the cheering must have been from his owner and trainer! The horse was draped in a blanket of roses and given a silver trophy as he stood in the winner's circle. A cash prize of $1,860,000 was also awarded. Not bad for a horse that cost $30,000.

This unlikely champion beat horses that had won far more races than he had won. The whole crew of owner, trainer, jockey, and horse were all equally unlikely to take part in such a victory. The triumph of Rich Strike would go down as the second biggest upset in Kentucky Derby racing history, proving that anything can happen and never give up on your dreams!

That Bear's Famous!

Bart worked alongside many famous actors, often stealing the show, despite never saying a word. How could this be?

Bart was an Alaskan Kodiak bear who was born in the Baltimore Zoo in 1977. He was adopted by trainers Doug and Lynne Seus when he was just a tiny, 5-pound fluffball, but he would grow in size to stand 9 and a half feet tall and weigh 1,500 pounds! Doug and Lynne are animal trainers that focus on working with grizzly bears. They train bears that follow commands and have easygoing behavior so that they can be used in movies and television. And it all started with Bart.

Bart's first movie was Windwalker, a 1981 western film. He went on to act in many other movies, including *The Edge, Legends of the Fall,* and Disney's *White Fang.* Bart would rub his bear elbows up against some of Hollywood's most famous actors including Brad Pitt, Sir Anthony Hopkins, and Ethan Hawke. They all had great respect for Bart and his ability to turn on his charm and his roar when needed.

Bart's greatest success came when he starred in the movie *The Bear.* He would finally have a leading role! In the movie, he played an adult bear who became friends with an orphaned cub. Together, they worked to defeat two trophy hunters. The film received international success and many people thought that Bart should be nominated for an Academy Award for Best Actor. At the time, animals were not allowed to be nominated.

Bart's opportunity to go to the Academy Awards wasn't over though. In 1998, Bart took part in the Academy Awards celebration honoring and recognizing animal actors. Bart even went onstage to hand an award envelope to Mike Myers, the voice of Shrek!

His trainers, Lynne and Doug, felt it was important to use Bart's influence to raise awareness for protecting the habitat of grizzly bears and other wildlife. They helped form the Vital Ground Foundation to educate people on bears, their habitats, and conservation. Bart was the "spokesbear" and he helped teach people about bear safety, keeping both people and bears safe.

Bart got cancer in 1998. He had several operations but eventually passed away at his home in Utah in 2000. He left behind a legacy of several other bears that Doug and Lynne trained for acting. He also left behind a growing group of people who are dedicated to keeping the grizzly bears and the lands they live in safe for years to come. While many people fear bears (and rightfully so) Bart used his skills and fame as a bear actor to help save the lives of many bears in the future.

Cow That Was Given
a Key to the City

On a cold February day in Cincinnati, Ohio, a cow took one look at her surroundings and her future and said, "Nope, not today!" She jumped a nearby 6-foot fence and made her way to freedom.

The cow, a middle-aged Charolais cow without a name, was standing at the slaughterhouse, waiting for her fate when she decided to take matters into her own hands. After clearing the fence and tasting freedom, she headed for safety. Nearby Mount Storm Park offered plenty of dense woods for her to avoid capture.

And it turns out she was really good at living in the wild! Despite their best efforts, local animal groups struggled with catching this cow. They used traps and even tried tranquilizer guns, but it was no use. This cow had won her freedom and she wasn't about to let it go.

By now, the whole city of Cincinnati had heard about the escaped cow and they were all rooting for her. Something about her determination and spunk caused a stir in the city. The Mayor, Charlie Luken, was rooting for her safe capture. He said he would give her a key to the city once she was apprehended.

Even with the whole city pulling for her, it just wasn't safe to have a loose cow this close to a big city.

She could cause a lot of problems if she were to get loose in traffic and no one wanted to see her or anyone else get hurt. So local officials kept pursuing the capture of this cow, whom the city was now lovingly calling Charlene Mookin, nicknamed after the mayor. After 11 days, she was finally captured just after midnight.

Her time on the run had come to an end, but what was the city going to do with a cow that was such an escape artist? After she had won the hearts of everyone in Cincinnati it was clear she could never go back to the slaughterhouse. The Cincinnati Zoo said they couldn't take her because they didn't have proper housing to contain this trickster cow.

That's when a special artist with a big heart stepped in. Peter Max, a famous artist, donated $180,000 worth of his original paintings to be sold. The money raised would go toward relocating the cow and allowing her to live out the rest of her days in safety on a farm with plenty of good grazing.

Peter took over ownership of the cow and renamed her Cincinnati Freedom or Cinci, for short. Before leaving the city for her retirement in the country, Cinci was given the Key to Cincinnati. She was supposed to be presented at the opening day parade for the Cincinnati Reds, but she was too nervous and jumpy to participate. They didn't want her to end up loose in the city again!

A few days later, Cinci moved to her forever home, an animal farm and sanctuary in New York state. The journey took 9 hours. When she was unloaded from the trailer, Cinci took in her surroundings and seemed to be pleased. She had plenty of other cow friends to graze with, including several other escapees. She became especially good friends with a cow named Queenie, who had escaped from a slaughterhouse in New York. Perhaps they had a lot to talk about!

Cinci was always a bit shy around humans but seemed to tolerate the many visitors that had heard her story and wanted to see her. She lived the rest of her life peacefully grazing and napping in sunny pastures. The farm workers said she would still occasionally jump their five-foot fences, but never wandered too far. I guess she just had a heart that liked to roam and loved a little bit of adventure!

Parrot Chatter Rescues a Little Girl in Trouble

Parrots are birds that are known for being able to talk or mimic certain words and sounds. Some parrots have a pretty extensive vocabulary, sometimes knowing and speaking up to a thousand words. Parrots have been known to have funny sayings that they repeat over and over again, as well as being able to mimic distinct sounds. They are pretty smart creatures.

While a parrot will often talk about things in a way that doesn't make sense, sometimes a parrot will be perfectly clear with the point they are trying to get across. Such is the case with a parrot named Willie. Willie is a Quaker parrot, a breed of bird that is well known for being chatty and intelligent. Quaker parrots typically have a vocabulary of 50-60 words. Willie lived with his owner Meagan. Also living with them were Meagan's friend Samantha and her daughter, Hannah.

Willie was excellent at entertaining anyone who would listen. He had a pretty extensive vocabulary, with "Silly Willie" being one of his favorite sayings. He was also a good mimic. He could imitate a dog, cat, chicken, and the sound of humans kissing. He could even whistle the theme song from *"The Andy Griffith Show."*

A few mornings a week, when Samantha had a class she attended, Meagan would babysit 2-year-old Hannah. One morning, while Samantha was at her class, Meagan was preparing a Pop-tart for Hannah while the toddler watched cartoons in the living room. Meagan put the Pop-tart on the counter to cool while she ran to the bathroom.

Meagan had been gone less than a minute when she heard the bird going crazy. He was shrieking, squawking, and flapping his wings. Then she heard something that made her panic. Willie kept screaming, " Mama. Baby. Mama. Baby," over and over again.

Meagan rushed into the living room where she found Hannah choking and holding half the uneaten Pop-tart in her hand. Hannah had climbed up onto the table to get to the Pop-tart but had choked on a large piece. Meagan grabbed the little girl and started doing the Heimlich maneuver until the food became dislodged.

Willie became quiet again as soon as Hannah was able to breathe. The flapping of wings and squawking of, "Mama. Baby," stopped. When Samantha came home and heard the story, she was incredibly grateful to Meagan for saving Hannah's life. But Meagan gave Willie all the credit, claiming that it was his loud, urgent squawking that moved her into quick action. Samantha was already a big fan of Willie but became an even bigger one after that.

One interesting tidbit was that although Willie knew the word *Mama*, he had never used it together with the word *Baby*. And since that day, he hasn't put the two words together again. It seemed like Willie knew the exact words that he needed to put together and use in order to get Meagan to save Hannah's life. What a smart, quick-thinking bird!

Elephant Empathy

Elephants are the largest animal in the world, weighing up to 14,000 pounds. Although they are usually peaceful animals, they can become aggressive if they are provoked. They also can become aggressive if they are injured or sick. And if an elephant is mad, watch out! They are so big that their anger can be dangerous.

A family was living in a small hut in India. The hut was fairly flimsy, meaning it was not that sturdy. Still, imagine the surprise of the family when an elephant crashed through the front door and wall! That's probably not something they were expecting.

The elephant was all by himself and was likely hungry and searching for food. When he crashed through the door he knocked down some of the walls and the ceiling. Wood and debris were everywhere. This angry elephant had made quite a mess!

But then something extraordinary happened. The family had a toddler that had been asleep in a bed near where the animal came through the wall. The family couldn't get to the baby and she started to cry loudly.

You would think that the loud noise might make the elephant even more upset and angry, but it did just the opposite. The elephant reached out his trunk to the little child. He used his trunk to remove the debris from the bed and clean up the mess. Then he turned and walked away, leaving everyone unharmed.

To the parents, this was incredible. They were so thankful that their child was untouched when she easily could have been killed. Elephants are known for being very empathetic animals. They are known to comfort their herd mates when they are suffering with chirps and rumbles. Elephants seem to understand feelings just like we do. And they respond with appropriate attitudes. It seems like these incredible animals are really just gentle giants.

Lulu the Hero

When Jo Ann and Jack Altsman agreed to babysit their daughter's pet pig, they weren't expecting to enjoy her as much as they did. But the pig, Lulu, became such a welcomed addition to their home that they asked if they could adopt her and let her live with them full time. This would end up being a lifesaving blessing for them!

Jo Ann was home by herself one day with Lulu and their dog, Bear, for company. Jack was out of town on a fishing trip. Suddenly, Jo Ann felt strange. She ended up collapsing on the floor because she was having a heart attack. Jo Ann yelled for help, but she was inside the house and no one could hear her. Bear became excited and began barking. Lulu must have known that she needed to do some quick thinking because she came up with a very clever plan.

Pigs are known for being incredibly intelligent animals. They also love their humans. Lulu's next move proves this fact. Lulu wanted to help Jo Ann and she seemed to know that she would need another human to do this. Lulu squeezed herself through the doggy door that was too small for her. She scraped herself because of the tight fit but didn't seem to care. She was a pig on a mission.

Outside, Lulu had never left the familiarity of her own yard, but today she bravely took off toward the road. She laid down on the road and waited. Surely someone would stop for this pig! Several cars drove right on by. Lulu went back and forth to the house several times to check on Jo Ann. Each time she went she had to squeeze through the narrow doggy door. Lulu ended up having many cuts and scrapes because of this. She was bleeding as she was laying on the road waiting for a helper to arrive.

A helper finally did arrive in the form of a driver who stopped to check on Lulu. He probably was afraid Lulu was dead! But when he got out of the car, Lulu hopped up. He could see that she was injured so he yelled toward the house. Lulu led him into the yard where the driver finally heard Jo Ann's cries for help. The driver quickly dialed 911 and medical attention was on the way.

When the medical team arrived, Lulu tried to get into the ambulance with Jo Ann. She wanted to be sure her human was ok! The medics gently pushed her out of the way and headed for the hospital. Jo Ann ended up needing open heart surgery. Doctors said that if she would have been without help for 15 minutes longer, she would have died. Lulu's quick thinking saved her owner's life!

While her owner was being taken care of, Lulu got her own wounds doctored. I'm sure it was a joyous reunion when Jo Ann finally got to come home from the hospital. Lulu became quite famous for her quick action and clever thinking. She was awarded a gold hero's medal from the American Society for the

Prevention of Cruelty to Animals. She even got to be a guest star on The Late Show with David Letterman and The Oprah Winfrey Show.

Lulu's intelligent and brave action saved her owner. Heroes can come in all shapes and sizes, even a giant pot-bellied pig!

A Tribute to Rufo

Sometimes, cities have a problem with stray animals, especially dogs and cats. It can be hard to take care of and find good homes for all these animals, especially if they are shy or skittish. One city in Spain had an interesting solution to a stray dog that took up residence on their streets.

No one really remembers how or when Rufo arrived in Oviedo, Spain but he certainly left his mark on the city. It was sometime in 1988 when people first remembered seeing the large dog. He was a mix of mastiff and german shepherd, so he was a pretty big guy. Although he didn't seem to have any special talents or abilities, he was extremely friendly and loved people. The people of the city loved him, too.

Over time, as the people around Oviedo became more and more fond of Rufo, it became apparent that he didn't have any owners to care for him. But by that point, it didn't matter because he seemed to be owned by all of the people around him. He lived on the streets but could always count on the people of the city to give him food, shelter, and whatever he needed. The City Council took over making sure he had his annual vaccinations and vet care. They would occasionally gather him up, take him to the vet, give him a bath and then release him back out onto the streets that he loved. He was owned by no one and he was owned by everyone. He knew where to go to find shelter when it was really hot or really cold. And he could always find someone willing to give him a good ear scratch and tell him he was a good boy.

Rufo would start most every day by arriving at 8 am at the local grocery store. After that, he would do whatever he pleased. Sometimes he would go to the park and watch soccer games. He liked to lay in an out-of-the-way spot and watch the people as they moved about with their lives in the city. He loved the nightlife in Oviedo and was often seen out at night socializing with people as they went out to dinner and dancing. One photographer from the city remembered seeing Rufo as he was heading home late one night. He and a friend took Rufo in for the night, fed him, and gave him a bath. Rufo seemed very happy to be allowed to come and go as he pleased. His needs were met, yet he had the freedom to explore the city that he loved.

If there was a big event, celebration, or ceremony in the city, you could be sure Rufo would be there. He was often found leading parades and marches and was even in the official photographs for some of the city's most important events. He once snuck into a special award ceremony at the fancy Campoamor Theater where he greeted the mayor. The mayor told him, "Rufo, I don't think you can do anything here." So Rufo turned and walked back outside.

On one occasion Rufo's friendliness got him into trouble. At a park, he was playing with another dog. The other dog bit a little girl, but by the time authorities arrived, the other dog was long gone. Rufo was apprehended and forced to go into quarantine. The city became outraged. There was even a demonstration where people gathered together demanding his release. Luckily, Rufo was found innocent and was not locked up for long.

As he got older, Rufo started to hang out with another dog friend. The people of the city noticed that he seemed to be getting more clumsy as he aged. They began to worry about his safety. A city official talked to the mayor about the situation. They agreed the best thing to do for Rufo would be to take him and his friend to the animal shelter. He lived there happily for several more years. They gave him the freedom to roam the yard and building, but this situation kept him safe as his eyesight began to fail.

Rufo died in 1997 and the city mourned their loss. To remember their friend, a statue was built. It looked just like Rufo and now everyone who had loved him could honor and remember him. The statue, whose head has become faded and worn from receiving so many pets, is a tribute not just to Rufo, but to all of the people everywhere who help abandoned animals.

Searching for Salamanders

Do you know what conservation is? It means to carefully maintain and protect something in nature to prevent it from disappearing. In Wisconsin, there is a special member of the conservation team at the Mequon Nature Preserve who helps to preserve the salamanders and protect the plants. Her name is Tilia and she is a chocolate labrador retriever.

How does a dog help with conservation? She uses one of her best attributes, her nose. Tilia's owner, Cory Gritzmacher, is the director of the nature preserve. All dogs are already equipped with about 200 million olfactory receptors in their nose. Olfactory receptors are the little things that help us with our sense of smell. People only have about 5 million of them which is a lot less than 200 million! Dogs are designed to be able to use their noses in ways humans can only imagine. But it takes quite a bit of training for dogs to use their noses in ways that humans can interpret.

The Mequon Nature preserve is on a mission to protect the wild salamanders that call the park home. These salamanders are elusive, meaning they are hard to find. These small amphibians are in trouble because of habitat loss and extreme climate variations. In order to protect the salamanders from becoming extinct, many conservationists are taking extra measures to help them. That's what makes Tilia's job so important.

Tilia can use her nose to sniff out the areas where the salamanders live. She searches the prairie's forests and wetlands and can alert her handler when she smells the salamanders. This helps her owner monitor the salamander population and do anything needed to help them thrive.

This also means keeping an eye on the invasive plants that can hinder the plants that they need. One such instigator is the wild parsnip. This plant spreads rapidly and chokes out many of the other plants in the area. In order to protect all of the other plants, the wild parsnip needs to be found in its first year, before it has seeded and grown. The problem is that in this early stage, it is close to the ground and often hidden by other plants, making it very hard for people to see. That's where Tilia and her nose come in handy.

Cory began Tilia's training as a puppy. She loves treats and loves searching for treats. When she initially began training, Cory started simple. He would put treats in cardboard boxes and let Tilia search for them. When she found a treat, she got to eat it as a reward. This led to pairing the scent of the salamander or wild parsnip with the treats. She would still be sniffing for the treat, but eventually, she began to associate the smell of salamander or wild parsnip with the treat. She didn't care what it smelled like, as long as she got her reward. When she is working in the field, she uses her nose to find the scent of wild parsnip or salamanders. When she does, her handler, Cory is sure to give her a treat that he carries in a pocket.

Cory says he thinks dogs are going to start to play a huge role in conservation efforts. "The best-trained volunteers or staff in the world won't even be able to find what a canine can," Gritzmacher said. "That's the pretty impressive part of it. And who doesn't want to go to work with a dog?"

The relationship between the dog and the handler plays a key role. Since Tilia can't talk, Cory has to be able to watch her body language for clues. He has to be able to know the difference between when she is following the correct scent or when she gets distracted by a deer or wild animal. And he has to be able to reward her quickly for a job well done. Nose work is hard work for dogs, and Tilia gets worn out after a day of being out in the field. Luckily, she gets to go home with Cory and doing her other job...being a family dog and getting lots of love.

Many people have heard of dogs that use their noses to sniff for drugs or bombs, but dog handlers are beginning to find many other interesting and helpful ways that dogs and their noses can benefit humans. Some dogs love having a job to do, and they can be trained to support their human handlers with specific tasks. Maybe we will see more and more dogs like Tilia helping with conservation efforts!

Ocean Safety Patrol

Dolphins are mammals that live in the ocean. They are extremely intelligent animals. They can communicate with each other using sound waves, clicks, and whistles. Dolphins are compassionate creatures and take care of other dolphins in their pod, all working together to find food and encourage any sick or injured dolphins.

With dolphins being so smart and helpful, it probably won't surprise you that there are many tales of dolphins rescuing humans in the ocean. They seem to come out of nowhere, and sometimes work with other members of their pod to save people.

Four swimmers in New Zealand were enjoying the water off the coast when a group of dolphins began to herd them all together. The dolphins were using their fins to slap the water while they circled the people rapidly. The circle became tighter and tighter. One of the swimmers, a lifeguard, tried to swim away from the group. Two of the larger dolphins pushed him back in. It was then that the lifeguard noticed a 12-foot great white shark heading right for them. The people would have certainly been in danger had the dolphins not been there to protect them. Luckily, the shark was deterred by the herd of dolphins and swam away.

Another story comes from the Red Sea. A group of twelve divers became separated from the boat that had taken them out to sea. They were stuck in the sea with no way to get to shore and no way to call for help. The divers were stranded for over 13 hours and a group of dolphins stayed with them the entire time. The dolphins protected them from predators. When a rescue boat finally appeared, the dolphins began to leap and jump in the air, as if to get the rescuers' attention.

There are stories of dolphins helping other creatures, too. A large group of pilot whales in New Zealand became trapped when the tide went out in the area where they were swimming. They were trapped in the shallow water until the tide came back in. Local people came down to the beach and took turns sponging the whales and trying to keep the upset whales calm. When the tide finally came back in, the whole ordeal had been so stressful that the whales were disoriented and didn't seem to know how to leave and reach safer waters. Luckily a group of dolphins nearby came to the rescue. They seemed to sense the danger of the situation and put themselves at risk by swimming into the shallow water. They encouraged the whales to follow them back out into the deeper ocean saving 76 trapped whales.

Researchers are still studying the reasons why dolphins seem to be so helpful and encouraging. Some researchers believe that dolphins seem to have a symbiotic relationship with humans. That means both species get something good from the relationship. Other researchers think it has to do with dolphins being able to use their sound waves, known as echolocation, to sense the human heartbeat. Sensing the heartbeat tells the dolphin when someone is scared. Much like a dolphin would protect a young dolphin or injured member of the pod, they also help humans.

Dolphins are fascinating mammals and it seems that marine biologists and other researchers are only beginning to discover the many fascinating things about them. I do know one thing, if I'm swimming in the ocean and a shark appears, I'm going to hope that a group of dolphins show up to rescue me!

Sergeant Reckless

Soldiers have to be brave. They face danger and uncertainty during times of war. They have to train hard and often take risks to help keep other soldiers safe and protect their country. Staff Sergeant Reckless was no exception. She was known for being fearless and valiant as she helped her fellow Marines during the Korean War. Yet, despite holding official military rank and being awarded top military honors, Reckless was no ordinary Marine. Why? Because Staff Sergeant Reckless was a horse!

The Marine's Recoilless Rifle Platoon was given permission to buy a pack horse to help carry the ammunition for their large rifles. The ammo was quite heavy with each shell weighing 24 pounds, and the platoon wanted to be capable of carrying 9 shells. A horse would be the perfect fit to help the soldiers with all of this heavy equipment.

Several of the Marines went to the racetrack in Seoul, Korea. There, they met their future friend and Marine, a chestnut 4-year-old mare (female horse). They bought her for $250 from a Korean boy who was selling her to help pay for a prosthetic leg for his sister.

Back at camp, the Marines named her Reckless, and began her training. They put her into "hoof camp" where they trained her not only on how to carry heavy loads, but how to stay safe in combat. Reckless was trained to avoid the barbed wire that seemed to be everywhere. She learned to lay down and get low when they were under fire. She even learned to run for a bunker if a Marine cried out "Incoming!" In the beginning, Reckless was kept in a pasture by the camp, but she soon became so friendly with everyone that she was allowed to roam the camp freely. She would often come into the Marines' tents to sleep and was even known for laying down next to the warm stove on cold nights.

Reckless had a big appetite and they soon learned not to leave food out or Reckless would eat it! She was particularly fond of Coca-Cola but was also caught eating bacon, eggs, toast, candy, peanut butter sandwiches, and mashed potatoes. Once, she even ate $30 worth of poker chips! Luckily, despite her habit of eating things that weren't always good for her, she didn't get sick.

Reckless adapted well to life with her platoon. She was a valuable team member. She really proved her worth during the Battle of Panmunjom-Vegas. This battle in 1953 lasted for three days. During one single day, Reckless carried over 9,000 pounds of ammunition for the Marines. She made 51 trips, all by herself, carrying the ammunition to the Marines who needed it. Throughout her travels, she covered over 35 miles and was injured twice. Once she was hit with shrapnel over her left eye and once on her left hip. But Reckless was brave. She could have stopped or run away during the battle. No one was there to make her keep working.

But she knew her job and loved helping the men she lived with.

For her courage, Reckless was promoted to Sergeant. She received two Purple Heart awards, as well as a Marine Corp Good Conduct Medal and several other honors. All of her awards were placed on a red and gold horse blanket with the Marine insignia.

By 1954 the war had ended and it was time for her platoon to be sent back home to California. But what would happen to Reckless? An article in the *Saturday Evening Post* asked the same question and the answer came quickly. An executive with a large company offered Reckless a ride back to America on one of his big ships.

So on November 10, 1954, Reckless arrived in California. This date is also the official birthday of the Marine Corps. She was invited to the Birthday Ball where she rode in an elevator and ate plenty of birthday cake, as well as some of the flower decorations. While at the event, Reckless wore her special red and gold blanket. This was actually her second blanket because she had eaten her first one!

Reckless lived at Camp Pendleton where she was well cared for and treated as royalty. She had a few noteworthy public appearances, but the Marines were careful to let her just be a horse. She had four babies while she was there. In 1959, Reckless was again promoted. She was now Staff Sergeant Reckless. During the ceremony, she was honored with a 19-gun salute and a parade of 1,700 Marines. Reckless was well loved by everyone!

This courageous little horse passed away at Camp Pendleton when she was about 20 years old. While she certainly wasn't the first animal to help the military during battle, she was one of the first animals to be honored with holding official military rank. Today, there are several statues honoring Reckless and her incredible bravery and determination. Animals are amazing!

Raccoons That (Might Have) Changed History

Raccoons are known for being naughty rascals. They love to eat, and these masked bandits have been known to cause all sorts of trouble with their huge appetites. They love to use their teeth for chompin' and chewin' but sometimes the snacks they choose aren't exactly appetizing. And every once in a while, a raccoon comes along whose mischief changes history.

It's hard to know if some of these tales are true or just raccoon folklore. After all, raccoons seem like the type of critters who would make up extravagant stories that place themselves as the main character.

Take, for example, a raccoon residing in Roanoke, Virginia during the Civil War. A letter was sent to General Robert E. Lee from a spy who worked for the Confederacy. The letter told exactly where a large Union battalion was. This information could mean a victory for the Confederate soldiers. However, a hungry raccoon somehow steals the letter and eats it before it makes it into the hands of General Lee. Without knowing what was stated in the letter, General Lee proceeds with his original plan. This leads to the Union winning the battle at Sailor's Creek and helped the Union win the war as well.

Years later, a young raccoon is in a tall tree in a park, climbing around and chattering. A boy named Jonas Salk watches, fascinated with the creature and his interaction with the world. The raccoon inspires the boy to investigate more with science. He eventually becomes a famous scientist, invents the groundbreaking polio vaccine, and saves the lives of many children. And it all started by watching a curious raccoon scampering around a tree.

Our next raccoon tale comes from Washington D.C. Rumor has it that the roof of the White House was needing repair. This was just after the Great Depression and Franklin D. Roosevelt is the President. America is trying to bounce back, but jobs need to be created for people to get back to work. Legend says a raccoon fell through the ceiling of the Oval Office as President Roosevelt was working on coming up with a plan for America. Somehow this inspired him. Perhaps he was thinking of needing workers to repair his roof! The Works Progress Administration was set in motion. This act put millions of people to work building public projects that included roads, libraries, public buildings, and even schools, and probably repairing the roof of the White House.

It's hard to prove whether these stories are true or just told in good fun, but something we can all agree on is the sneaky, shifty ways raccoons seem to find trouble. Whether they are sneaking around in trash cans, stealing food out of gardens, or snatching shiny objects from someone's porch, raccoons are a special kind of animal. These masked critters have a way of coming around when we least expect them, so it's entirely possible that they were there to make their mark on history!

Life Changing Bob

James Bowen was down on his luck in 2007. He was in his mid-twenties, living in London, and struggling to find his way in life. He often felt like he didn't have a purpose and couldn't find a job he loved. He was often homeless. His sadness led him to make poor decisions. His life was in a very dark place.

Sometimes, even when we are very troubled, hope comes along in ways we are not expecting it. That's exactly what happened to James. He returned to his small apartment one night to find an orange cat outside his door. He assumed the cat belonged to a neighbor, but the cat was still there the next morning. Bob noticed that the cat was very skinny and dirty. The cat also had a cut on his leg that looked infected. Nobody in his apartment building claimed the cat, but one lady knew where James could take it to the vet. At the vet, the cat was given some medicine to help the cut on his leg heal. James used his last $20 to pay for the medicine for his new friend.

At home, James still assumed the cat belonged to somebody else. He looked for the owner but kept the cat in his apartment so he could be sure he received his medicine every day. When the medicine was gone, James released the cat outdoors, assuming he would go back home. But the cat stayed. He began meeting James at the door and following him everywhere...even onto the bus! It seemed as though James had a new cat. He decided to name him Bob.

Bob loved going everywhere with James. He would often ride on his shoulders and they became a familiar sight around the neighborhood they lived. At this point, James decided that he would stop doing things that were bad for him, like drugs. He wanted more out of his life with his new cat, Bob, and he wanted to know Bob would always get good care. James entered treatment to get help and was able to clean up his life.

James wanted to keep Bob safe, so he bought a little harness so that Bob would stay close to him when they traveled. James was a street performer and he would let Bob come along to certain areas where he would perform. James also sold newspapers on the London streets with Bob helping him attract customers. James and Bob's fan base grew. The public loved Bob and even tourists to London would visit them.

A newspaper reporter did an article on James and Bob. This led to James being offered a book deal to write a book about his life with Bob. The book was released in 2012 and quickly became a bestseller in Britain. It was followed by three more books about Bob. Altogether, the books sold over 8 million copies and were printed in forty languages. A lot of people really liked Bob!

The books were so successful that some movie directors wanted to turn them into a movie. In 2016, *A Street Cat Named Bob* was released starring Bob as himself! Bob got to meet members of the royal family at the movie premiere. It even won an award for Best British Film.

Mostly, James and Bob just lived a normal life together. James said Bob was a free spirit and very smart. He learned how to open doors and was even known for using the toilet in James' apartment! The two were always together and enjoyed each other's company.

Sadly, Bob passed away in 2020. He was at least 14 years old. Bob gave friendship and companionship to James when he needed it the most. He didn't judge James for his bad decisions, instead, he inspired him to make himself better and get his life back on the right track. James said, "Bob saved my life. It's as simple as that."

Animals can be such wonderful friends and seem to always want to cheer us up and make us feel better. What an incredible gift of friendship James and Bob were able to give each other for all of their years together.

Grumpy Cat

On April 4th, 2012, a kitten was born that would change internet history...at least for cats. That's right. This was the birthday of Grumpy Cat.

Her name was Tardar Sauce, and she was born with a form of feline dwarfism, giving her a few distinct features, such as an underbite (her lower jaw was set further back than her upper teeth), a flat face, and bubble eyes. The result? She appeared to have a permanent grumpy expression on her face. She also had back legs that were shorter than her other legs, giving her a bit of a wobble when she walked.

On September 22, 2012, Tardar Sauce's family released a photo of her on the internet. The photo showed her precious, but grumpy-looking face. People went crazy over it. In the first 48 hours, the photo had over 1 million views. People began using the photo to make funny memes. When someone suggested the cat's picture might have been photoshopped, Tardar Sauce's family made a Youtube video to prove she was real. The Youtube video also received millions of views. A cat star was born. Even though her family said she was a very sweet and happy cat, everyone loved her permanently grumpy expression.

With her new fame, Tardar Sauce began to get requests for public appearances. She was "interviewed" on the *Today* show and *Good Morning America*. Her big break came when she was asked to attend South by Southwest, a popular film, media, and music festival in Austin, Texas. Friskies, a cat food company, hired her as a spokescat for their brand. They offered to fly her out to the festival. She and her owner flew first class, and she enjoyed all the benefits of being a star. She got a private room with a king-sized bed, a personal assistant, a chauffeur, and all the Friskies kitty food she could want.

At the South by Southwest festival, Tardar Sauce made 2-hour appearances daily where she appeared as Grumpy Cat. She was the biggest star of the event, drawing bigger crowds than Elon Musk, former Vice President Al Gore, and author Neil Gaiman. The line to meet Grumpy Cat was hours long and stretched three city blocks!

After the festival, Grumpy Cat's popularity continued to grow. Memes and internet videos of her cute but grumpy face spread, and so did the smiles of everyone who saw her. She had appearances on several network television talk shows and even promoted a book, featuring herself as Grumpy Cat! She was interviewed for Forbes magazine, where the reporter and Grumpy Cat sat across from each other in red velvet chairs. How fancy! In 2014, Grumpy Cat even got to star in a movie about herself, Lifetime's *Grumpy Cat's Worst Christmas Ever.*

Her owners were able to use her picture to sell things with her face on them. The Grumpy Cat brand is now worth millions of dollars.

Tardar Sauce passed away in her family home in 2019. Her owners said she was a cherished member of their family and she will be remembered for making so many people smile. I think the lesson this cute cat teaches us is to just be ourselves. Even our imperfections are beautiful.

Eagle Huntress

In 2016, 13-year-old Aisholpan Nurgaiv of Mongolia broke down barriers that had been in place for over 2,000 years. Aisholpan was the first girl to ever compete in the Golden Eagle Festival in Mongolia. And she didn't just compete, she WON!

In the mountains of western Mongolia, the Kazakh people are nomadic. They raise goats and cattle and often hunt to provide food and furs to use or trade. A long-standing tradition amongst the Kazakh people is hunting with golden eagles. It is practiced in everyday life and celebrated at competitions. Boys begin to learn the process at around 13 years of age. They work for their fathers or other men in the community learning the art of connecting with their eagle and using that bond to hunt.

Even as a young girl, Aisholpan was fascinated with the eagles. She used to help her father care for his eagle and seemed to have a natural gift for it. As she grew older and was taking on more responsibility in the household, her father decided to go against over 2,000 years of tradition. He began to train Aisholpan as a golden eagle hunter when she was 10 years old.

Her father was a very good eagle hunter. He taught Aisholpan how to do well in the sport. But dedication and drive are big parts of who she is. She loves her eagle, White Wings, and the bond they share.

The eagles are not born in captivity. Instead, they are taken from nests in the wild. Although this may seem cruel to us, to the Kazakh people, they are in a community with the eagles and the eagles are eventually released back into the wild. They believe that no one owns the eagles.

Aisholpan chose and took her own eagle when she was just a chick. She named her White Wings for the feathers on her wings. The eagles live with the family and so they forge strong bonds. Just like people, they have good moods and bad moods, and an important part of handling and hunting with these birds is being able to read them.

On a hunting day, the hunters ride out on their ponies with the eagles until they reach a ridge or valley where they can have an excellent view. When a fox, rabbit, or some other prey is spotted, the rider will surge forward and release the eagle. The beauty of the hunt is in the unpredictability of nature. You can't make the eagle hunt. It has to have the desire and drive to perform the task. If the hunt is goes well, the meat and fur will be used for the family for food and clothing.

The Golden Eagle Festival is an old tradition held every year to show off the skills of the eagles and trainers. There are usually around 40 men and boys who compete. In 2016, Aisholpan became the very first girl competitor. Although initial sentiments about a girl competitor were skeptical, after seeing Aisholpan and her ability to train and bond with White Wings, she won over the hearts of many and dramatically won the contest!

When an eagle reaches maturity (usually around 4-7 years old depending on the bird) the Kazakh people feel it is only right to release them back into the wild. This can be an emotional process as the trainer and bird have worked together for years. The ritual includes leaving the bird a deceased sheep to feed upon. In their community, an offering of a sheep is used when saying goodbye to a family member. The bird is released into the wild, already knowing how to hunt and fend for itself. The hunter eventually will select another chick to train and the process starts over.

For the people of Mongolia, many factors are changing what have been old traditions with eagle hunting. Many of these changes have to do with extreme weather making hunting more difficult as well as the decline in interested hunters. But as long as there are girls and boys like Aisholpan who are allowed to keep competing and training their golden eagles, the sport will continue to be practiced amongst the Kazakh people.

The Wealthiest Animals in the World

When she hatched from an egg and entered this big, beautiful world, the chicken, Gigoo, didn't know what an adventure was waiting for her in life.

Gigoo is a Scots Dumpey chicken, which is a Scottish breed known for having unusually short legs so that the chicken's body sits just centimeters off the ground. But this is not the most astonishing thing about Gigoo.

Gigoo belonged to Miles Blackwell and his wife. The Maxwells were owners of a very successful book publishing company. The year before, they had sold their interest in the company and retired to the English countryside. They loved being outdoors and wanted to breed farm animals that were not as common, such as Scots Dumpey chickens and the spiral-horned Manx Loghtan sheep. Continuing the bloodlines of these rare farm animals was an important and enjoyable endeavor for them.

Sadly, Miles' wife passed away when she was only 46 years old. Miles died unexpectedly just three weeks later. They never got to fully see their dreams of a long life living in the country with their farm animals come true.

So what happened with all the money the couple had made during their years running a successful business? Usually, when someone dies, their money goes to their children or other important family members. But the Blackwells didn't have any children. They left $42 million dollars to different charities that helped support the arts, music, the environment, and even rare farm animals.

Here's where things get fun. The Blackwells had an additional $15 million left to give. In their will, they left $15 million to their chicken, Gigoo. That's right! Fifteen million dollars!

Gigoo is now the richest animal alive. I'll bet she is living it up on a fancy farm somewhere eating the finest chicken feed available!

Gigoo may be the wealthiest, but she is not the only animal to inherit money from an owner. An Italian property owner left $13 million dollars to her cat to make sure he was well cared for after her death. The cat had once been a stray cat. Talk about moving up in the world! And speaking of strays, a street cat named Tinker won the heart of a lady he used to visit. When she died, she left him her $800,000 house and a $226,000 trust to provide him with everything he needed for his upkeep.

It is definitely important to always take care of pets, even making sure that they are cared for after the owners have died. That's what a responsible pet owner should do. We all love animals, it just seems that some people go further than others in what that looks like. Or maybe their pets just have really expensive tastes!

Six More Weeks of Winter

On February 2nd, he's either the most popular or unpopular rodent around depending on his actions. I'm talking about Punxsutawney Phil, the star of Groundhog's Day!

Phil is a groundhog, sometimes called a woodchuck, who lives in Punxsutawney, Pennsylvania. On Groundhog's Day, legend has it that he will emerge from his hibernation spot. If he sees his shadow he will go back into his den and we can expect 6 more weeks of winter. If he doesn't see his shadow we can celebrate because spring is here!

The first recorded Groundhog's Day happened in Punxsutawney in 1886, although the celebration was likely happening before then. Since then, the annual gathering has grown. Prior to 1993, the festival that is celebrated in honor of Groundhog's Day was fairly small, mostly attracting local people. After the release of the popular comedy movie *Groundhog's Day* in 1993, the size of the festival has grown a bunch. Most years the event attracts between 10,000-20,000 visitors to watch Phil perform his task.

The festival starts in the wee hours of the morning before any groundhog has even thought about getting up. Bussing to the event starts at 3 am. Most of us are still in bed at that hour! Spectators gather at Gobbler's Knob, the special place in the park where the big event takes place. There is a stage and everything. There is a pre-selected group of people known as the "Inner Circle" who are responsible for following the many traditions that have been set over the years. These men wear tophats and tailcoats, so they look very official.

The vice-president of the group has a big job before the event. He prepares two scrolls: one that states that there will be six more weeks of winter and one that proclaims an early spring. Legend has it that only the President of the Inner Circle, who holds the rare acacia wooden cane, is able to communicate with Phil. He and Phil communicate using the very official language of Groundhogese. I'm not making this up! As the sun starts to come up on Groundhog's Day, Phil awakens from sleep and leaves his burrow. He is helped to the top of a tree stump by the Inner Circle. Phil and the Inner Circle President communicate over his prediction. Everyone waits with bated breath. Will it be spring? Or will there be more winter?

In past history, Phil has guessed that it would be spring only 20 times. He has predicted more winter 105 times. It seems to me like the Pennsylvania winters might have something to do with it, but I can't speak Groundhogese. Estimates guess that Phil's accuracy rating is usually only 35-40 percent right. But don't tell that to the Inner Circle, who claim Phil is always 100 percent right.

After the momentous declaration from Phil, the crowd flocks back down the hill from Gobbler's Knob to partake in a day of fun festivities. Phil probably goes back to bed. Most groundhogs are not actually done hibernating on February 2nd.

During the year, our buddy Phil lives with his wife Phyllis at a small zoo where they live in a man-made burrow. The burrow has a viewing window, so tourists can admire the famous groundhog when they visit the zoo.

Groundhogs out in the wild typically live to be about 6 years old. But Phil is 136 years old. How can that be? The Inner Circle claims that Phil drinks an "elixir of life" every summer at the Groundhog Picnic. Sounds a little fishy to me! But it just adds to the fun and hoopla of Groundhog's Day.

Groundhogs are small rodent-like creatures that can be found across North America. They are very helpful in keeping the soil healthy. Groundhogs can swim or climb trees when they feel threatened but they prefer to go to their burrow to feel safe. They mostly eat grasses and berries. Occasionally they will eat small animals, grasshoppers, and snails. Groundhogs usually dig a winter burrow and sleep in it from October to March. When they hibernate, their body temperature can drop to 35 degrees and their heart rate lowers to only 4-10 beats per minute. Their breathing slows, so they only breathe once every 6 minutes! Male groundhogs usually emerge before the females, so you would likely see Phil before Phyllis.

Next Groundhog's Day you will have a lot of cool information to share with your friends. Or make a trip to visit Phil and see the entire thing for yourself!

Is That a Mermaid?

A long time ago, Christopher Columbus and his crew were sailing the seas and searching for new land. On the horizon, the sailors thought they saw an elusive creature they had only heard about from other sailors. They had seen the writings and drawings that were common during this time. They were just sure they were seeing mermaids, female figures with fish bodies swimming in the ocean. But they weren't quite what they expected. Christopher Columbus even wrote in his journal:

> "...when the Admiral went to the Rio del Oro [Haiti], he said he quite distinctly saw three mermaids, which rose well out of the sea; but they are not so beautiful as they are said to be, for their faces had some masculine traits."

Early sailors weren't seeing mermaids. They were very likely seeing manatees! Manatees are large mammals that live in the sea. Their bodies resemble that of the walrus and they are sometimes called sea cows. The manatee's closest relative is actually the elephant. Manatees and elephants both have thick skin with wrinkles, along with hair lightly covering their body. While some elephants can weigh up to 14,000 pounds, most manatees weigh around 1000 pounds.

Ok, but how were the sailors confusing these sea cows with mermaids? I mean, it doesn't seem that hard to tell them apart. You have to remember that back in those days, they didn't have television and computers filling their heads with what mermaids might look like. They were only going by what people had said these mysterious things looked like. And they had heard about these figures that floated up close to the surface of the water and bobbed around. Plus, it's very likely these sailors were exhausted and dehydrated. Not exactly thinking straight!

Manatees do float up close to the surface of the water. In fact, they have to do this to breathe. Manatees go to the surface every 3-5 minutes to refill their lungs with oxygen. When they do this they refill their lungs 90 percent. Humans only refill to about 10 percent. Manatees can actually hold their breath underwater for about 20 minutes but usually come up more frequently.

Here's a fun fact. Manatees are buoyant, meaning they can float. How do they control this buoyancy? Through their farts! If they want to float to the surface, farting will help the manatee be able to come up to the surface for air. And while manatees may look like they are super fat with their big tummies, their midsection is packed full of stomach and intestines. Manatees actually don't have much blubber to keep them warm. This is why they prefer to live in warm, tropical regions.

Manatees lose their teeth often and unlike humans and most other mammals, they regrow their teeth continually throughout their life. Their diet is mostly made up of grasses and they will graze on seagrass and freshwater plants for about 7 hours a day. Manatees aren't very fast swimmers. They only travel at speeds of about 3-5 miles an hour. This puts them in danger of boat traffic as they can't get out of the way fast enough.

In fact, unlike the open seas when Columbus and his crew were sailing the ocean blue, manatees are actually in danger. Boat traffic, pollution, and colder winter water temperatures put today's manatees at risk. They are actually listed as being vulnerable to extinction. Wildlife and ocean conservation groups are working hard to find ways to protect these cute creatures. Mermaids may not be real, but manatees certainly are and we'd like for them to be around for a long time!

The Magpie that Helped
a Family Heal

In 2013, Sam Bloom's life changed forever. The vivacious mother of three young boys loved to surf and participate in ocean sports. The Australian family took a vacation to Thailand that would change their lives. Sam was up on a balcony that collapsed and sent her falling 40 feet to the ground. The fall left her paralyzed from the chest down. The once active adventurer was now confined to a wheelchair. She spent 7 months in the hospital undergoing intense rehab and therapy. But life would never be the same.

Sam struggled with the sudden and tragic change in her life. She didn't know how to channel her emotions now that she couldn't be active. Her home seemed different and less welcoming when viewed from her wheelchair. She was in a dark place and having trouble finding her purpose and any sense of happiness.

Three months after returning from the hospital, Sam's family was visiting her mother's house. Her oldest son, Noah, found a magpie chick in the park who had been injured when she fell 65 feet out of her nest. A magpie is a type of extremely intelligent bird. They are about the size of a large crow and are known for being good songbirds.

Sam and Noah wanted to help this little chick. They took it home where they created a small habitat for her using a laundry basket and some soft blankets. They spoke with several veterinarians to get advice on the best way to feed the chick. Magpie babies eat a lot of insects, more than the Bloom family could possibly find, so they were advised to create a paste of high protein ingredients. They would hold the paste in their fingers, just above the little bird's head and she would reach up and eat, just as she would with her mother bird. She needed to be fed every two hours during the daytime but luckily would sleep through the night.

The family decided to name the bird Penguin because she was black and white and she waddled when she walked. Penguin's life was touch and go for a while and sometimes the Blooms weren't sure she was going to make it. But little by little she got stronger. Pretty soon she was able to hop up onto a branch that they had connected to her basket.

As Penguin got stronger, so did Sam and the whole Bloom family. The sadness in the house seemed to subside. Penguin made them laugh and Sam felt like she had a purpose in helping the bird thrive. Life started to feel normal again. And having a bird was fun. Penguin didn't act like a normal bird, as she had essentially been raised by humans. When Penguin started to fly, she was known for flying into bed for cuddles. She would even roll onto her back to snuggle. Because they were together all day long, Penguin and Sam shared a special bond.

When Penguin was old enough, the family began to let her go outside. They never wanted her to feel trapped. But she still preferred to sleep inside with the family, usually in her basket where she felt safe. As she got older, she had to live outside full-time. She wasn't potty trained and was constantly taking small things in the house and moving their location. That is a common trait in magpies, but can be difficult in a home! Even when she was outside, Penguin was still a member of the family. She would sit in a certain tree and wait every day for the kids to get home from school. When the bus arrived she would sing a song. Often she would fly into the house if she found a window open!

As Penguin got older, she began to leave the Bloom's yard for weeks at a time but would come back on occasion to visit. She once came back on one of the son's birthdays even though they hadn't seen her for weeks. In 2015, she disappeared for good. Magpies are resilient birds and can live for 25-30 years. They hope she is out in the world thriving and maybe has even started her own family.

The Bloom family said that although many people think they rescued Penguin, in many ways Penguin rescued them. She brought happiness and joy back into the house. Sam found a way to get back into the water sports that she loved, even competing in adaptive surfing and paracanoeing. There is a book and a movie adaptation of this story called *Penguin Bloom*.

The Grinch That Ate Christmas

A couple living in Ottawa, Canada was pretty excited about Christmas. They bought three 150 light strands and used them to decorate their back fenceline, giving it lots of holiday cheer. This was an area that they had decorated every year for thirty years. But this year was different. Within a few weeks, the lights stopped working. Upon further inspection, Mr. McCabe found that the wires had been chewed through in several places and several bulbs were missing.

Who was the mystery villain? Squirrels. Very curious, and apparently hungry squirrels had destroyed the Christmas cheer. The next year, the McCabe's tried decorating in a different place. The backyard fence line had a lot of squirrel activity, it was practically a squirrel highway! So they arranged the decorations on their back deck. Again, a few weeks in and the lights stopped working. That was about $200 worth of Christmas lights, down the drain...all due to squirrel shenanigans!

A big park in St. Paul, Minnesota had the same problem. Squirrels chewed through so many of the city's elaborate park displays that the event coordinator refused to put up a big Christmas decoration display the following year. The city's display cost around $27,400 for all the lights, a large sum of money that the event coordinator didn't want to part with just to have squirrels destroy them. "It was a constant battle," volunteer John Mannillo said. "We'd have to go in and repair the lights every week. We'd come in and there'd be two or three trees out."

In Cincinnati, Ohio these rodents seem to be at war with the workers at the Cincinnati Zoo. "They wreak havoc here at the zoo," said an employee. Not only are they getting into trash cans and eating tulip bulbs in the spring, but the squirrels also seem to have developed a taste for the zoo's LED Christmas light display for their Festival of Lights.

Are squirrels really against Christmas? Probably not. Squirrels are just naturally born chewers. A squirrel's teeth are constantly growing, so they have to chew on things to keep their teeth worn down. While squirrels usually chew on twigs or small sticks, it seems that some squirrels love the taste of plastic.

Many Christmas light companies coat their wires in polylactic acid, a derivative of corn syrup. So it could be that the wires are just plain tasty! Many people have struggled to keep squirrels out of their flower and vegetable gardens, but no one really expected they would have to discourage them from eating Christmas decorations. Some people even believe that the squirrels might think the Christmas bulbs are acorns and they are just storing them away. Somewhere, there is a squirrel that has a very colorful "acorn" collection.

Christmas decor lovers will continue to try anything in their battle against the squirrels. The park in Minnesota changed its light display to include more projector lights that give the squirrels less edible possibilities. The McCabe's in Canada opted to move their decoration indoors. And as for the Cincinnati Zoo, they have a few different tactics. One is hot sauce. It seems the little rodents might have a taste for plastic but they don't like the spicy sauce with it. Another strategy is to leave the Christmas lights on. When a squirrel takes a bite of wire, he gets a jolt of electricity that will surely make him and his friends rethink their Christmas feast!

It seems that as long as we enjoy Christmas lights and squirrels enjoy chewing, there will be someone who is in a Christmas light conflict with these furry gray critters!

How a Tiny Dog Turned Into a Worldwide Hero

Tiny Patron weighs less than 9 pounds, but he's made a huge impact in helping people rebuild after the Russian invasion of Ukraine. Patron is a Jack Russell Terrier, a breed of dog that was originally used for fox hunting. This breed of dog is known for being fast, energetic, and having a keen sense of smell.

So what does Patron do that makes him so famous? Patron has been trained to help find bombs and other explosives that were left behind during the Russian invasion of Ukraine. His owner, Mykhailo Iliev, works for the Civil Protection Service. Part of his job is to search for these explosives so that they can be safely removed and destroyed so no more citizens get hurt.

Patron, a name that means ammo in Ukrainian, was bought by Mykhailo to be a pet for his son. But as Patron started to travel to work with his new owner, it became apparent that he had a real knack for using his nose. So Mykhailo put him to work and trained him to sniff for gunpowder. Exploring wooded areas and farmland, Patron can sniff along and use his nose to detect the gunpowder, alerting his owner of an explosive device. The bombs are then neutralized, meaning they are no longer dangerous. They are then moved to an area to be safely destroyed. Patron has located over 250 explosives and he is just getting going! Mykhailo thinks that they probably have at least three more years worth of work to explore areas and make sure they are safe.

Patron has a little vest he wears when it is time to go to work. When his vest is off, he likes to act like any other dog. He likes to run and he LOVES to dig. But when his vest comes out, Patron is all business. His small size lets him go into areas that are too small for people and even most other bomb-sniffing dogs. Most of the explosive devices have been pre-set to explode with pressure over 11 pounds. Being tiny and weighing less than 9 pounds certainly gives this little guy the advantage, and it keeps him safe.

Patron has even been awarded a medal from the Ukrainian president Volodymyr Zelensky. At the ceremony, he got to meet the visiting Canadian Prime Minister. Wow, this dog has met some important people! For his service to humanity, Patron was also awarded the Palm Dog Award at the famous Cannes Film Festival.

Patron is working hard and doing another important job. In addition to finding all of these explosive devices, Patron is making sure children are aware of the dangers of these explosives. Patron has become a huge hit, especially in Ukraine, and he is teaching kids to stay aware and be safe. With so many bombs left behind, it is important that kids know what they look like and not play with them.

Patron has become a hero. People around the world have been following his story. This is important to the people of Ukraine as they are trying to safely rebuild areas that were damaged. Patron's Instagram page has over 220,000 followers! That's one popular dog.

So what does this doggie hero like to do when he is off duty? He likes to unwind with his family. He has been known to go visit sick children in the hospital to help lift their spirits. He loves to get a good belly rub. And he is crazy about cheese! Do you think he gets lots of cheesy treats for being such a good dog? I sure hope so.

Elephant Saves a Girl From a Deadly Tsunami

Amber Owen and her family were on an incredible month-long family vacation to Phuket, Thailand when one of the world's deadliest natural disasters hit. Amber was incredibly lucky that she survived this terrible event, all thanks to an elephant that had become her friend.

December 26, 2004, started out just like every other day of their vacation for Amber. She grabbed a few bananas and headed down to the beach at the resort where she and her family were staying. On the beach, the resort had elephants and the handlers would give rides to the children every morning. Amber had become particularly fond of one elephant named Ning Nong. She refused to ride any other elephant and would always share bananas with Ning Nong.

As Amber rode Ning Nong on the beach that morning no one knew of the disaster that was about to happen. A fierce earthquake occurred under the ocean floor causing a giant wave to build along the ocean's surface. This wave turned into a giant tsunami traveling as fast as 500 miles per hour. In some places, the wave was 100 feet high! Not long after the earthquake occurred, the tsunami was hitting land, meaning that no one had any time to prepare or react.

The tsunami affected 14 different countries, reaching coastal towns all over the Indian Ocean. The tsunami and the aftereffects, such as the flooding, resulted in the loss of nearly 230,000 lives.

But on the beach, eight-year-old Amber was just enjoying the morning and an elephant companion. So she thought it was weird when the elephant began to act a little odd. Usually, the elephant loved to wade with Amber into the water. But today, she kept heading inland, despite her handler encouraging her otherwise.

One small sign of a tsunami is that the ocean will recede. This means that the water on the beach will be pulled away from the land and back out into the depths of the ocean. This happened on the beach in Phuket, but it was such a rare occurrence that people didn't know what it meant.

As the water receded and people gathered on the beach to observe it, Ning Nong seemed to know that things weren't safe. With Amber on her back and her handler hanging on to her ropes, Ning Nong began to run to higher ground. When the wave hit she was a safe enough distance away that the strong elephant didn't get sucked back out to sea. She turned and stood her ground, fighting amongst the turbulent waters to reach safety.

Amber gripped the elephant tightly, watching in horror as people on the beach were swept up into the giant wave. Ning Nong finally reached a safe location and Amber was able to get down. Amber's mother was not on the beach when the wave hit. She ran out when she was able, looking for Amber and the elephant. She was so relieved to find them together, knowing that if Amber hadn't been riding Ning Nong, she likely would have drowned.

Amber and Ning Nong's story is an incredible tale of how animals have instincts that can be quite different from humans. In some cases, it would probably be a good idea for us to slow down and pay attention to what animals are trying to tell us!

I'll Be Your Eyes

Morris Frank was born and raised in Nashville, Tennessee in the early 1900s. He had a normal childhood until age 6 when he was riding his horse and went under a tree branch. He got poked in the eye by a stick and lost sight in that eye. Coincidentally, his mother had lost sight in her eyes as well, in an unrelated event. Morris helped his mother and understood the difficulties that she faced. All was well until he was 16 years old. Morris was practicing boxing with a friend and got punched in the face. He lost his vision in his other eye and was now completely blind.

Life is hard for the vision impaired now, but it was even more difficult back then. There were fewer options for help. Morris had once been an extremely active person, but now he was struggling to find his way in this new and very dark world. Four years after his second accident, his father read him a newspaper article about Dorothy Eustis. Dorothy was an American dog trainer who was living in Sweden and training dogs to help soldiers who had become vision impaired because of the war. Morris was intrigued. He had never heard of this type of work being done before. He wrote to Dorothy and asked if he could train with her and if they could educate dog trainers in the United States on how to train and work with guide dogs. "Help me and I will help them. Train me and I will bring back my dog and show people here how a blind man can be absolutely on his own," he wrote in his letter.

Dorothy contacted Morris and asked him to come to Sweden. The guide dogs she was working with were German Shepherd dogs. Morris was given a dog named Kiss, whom he immediately renamed Buddy. Morris and Buddy bonded and worked hard to learn how to work as a team for the five weeks they were in Sweden. Then Morris and Buddy headed back to the United States to be ambassadors for guide dogs and the blind.

They arrived in New York City and quickly caught the attention of the media. Morris and Buddy demonstrated how with the help of a guide dog, a blind person could get around independently. They showed this by crossing West Street and later Broadway in New York City, both very busy and dangerous streets. As the story began to spread and interest in guide dogs grew, Morris composed a one-word telegraph to Dorothy, which simply stated "Success."

A year later Morris and Dorothy opened the first school for guide dogs. It was called The Seeing Eye. At the school, the first classes were held and blind people were paired with their seeing-eye dogs. Morris and Buddy traveled the country sharing their story and acting as ambassadors for the school and for guide dogs. As people started to see the success of blind people and their new dogs, attention for the school and guide dog support spread.

Guide dogs are extremely well trained and have to be alert. They help their person get to where they want to go. Sometimes they have to practice what is known as intelligent disobedience. This is when the dog sees something the handler can't see and therefore can't complete the task the handler wants to do. Perhaps the dog sees that there is something unsafe in its path. The guide dogs are trained to alert their handler of steps, traffic, and where to find doors. These are some smart dogs! They are trained to travel in straight lines for the benefit of their blind handler.

Morris said that with Buddy by his side, he was able to get his life back. He had envied how on the street, two people with their sight could easily stop and strike up a conversation. But with Buddy by his side, it became easy and natural for people to inquire about his dog, making conversation easy for this once lonely blind man.

Morris and Dorothy's guide dog school that was started all those years ago is still training dogs today and is one of the largest in the country. They have paired over 16,000 people with dogs that have changed their lives for the better. Guide dogs give blind or impaired people the freedom to do the things that they weren't able to do before they met their guide dog partner. They help them become more independent and lead more normal lives, less hindered by their vision impairment than they once were. And, of course, these dogs offer the utmost companionship and friendship. Guide dogs are incredibly loyal and dedicated to their owners. Many guide dogs become loving members of the family.

Thanks to a dedicated dog trainer, a determined blind man, and a German Shepherd named Buddy, guide dogs have been serving people in the US for nearly 100 years. What a life-changing experience that has shaped the future for so many people. These pioneers in their field have helped generations of people to live independent lives no longer restricted by their vision impairment.

Gone To The Dogs

With a name like Rabbit Hash, Kentucky, you can be sure that this is one interesting place. But you are about to think it's even cooler. That's because Rabbit Hash has had a dog for its mayor since 1998.

Rabbit Hash is a small town in north-central Kentucky with a population of a little over 300 people. And it seems that all of these people feel that a canine is a better candidate than a human for the town mayor. The name Rabbit Hash is said to date back to 1847 when a historic flood sent the rabbits in the area searching for higher ground. The rabbits became a staple in the townspeople's diet as they were so plentiful. Steamboats on the Ohio River used to stop so the boat operators could eat the famous rabbit hash that gave the town its namesake.

But what does that have to do with a dog mayor? The idea came along in 1998 when a citizen thought that it would be really fun to elect some type of animal for the first mayor of the town. That's right, this town has never had an actual human mayor!

The event started as a fundraiser for the town's historical society. The people of Rabbit Hash could "vote" for their favorite mayoral candidate. Each vote costs $1 and unlike most elections, people are encouraged to vote more than once. The winner of the 1998 election was Goofy Borneman, a mixed-breed dog who died while in office. He was 16 years old when he passed away.

The mayor's position remained vacant until 2004 when Junior Cochran, a black labrador retriever was elected. There was a bit of scandal around Junior. He had gotten into trouble for entering the town's popular general store, even though no dogs were allowed. The dog's owners and other loyal supporters tried to get a "mayoral exemption" for this ban, but could never get it to pass. It seems even the mayor of Rabbit Hash had to follow the "No Dogs Allowed" rule.

Lucy Lou, a black and white border collie became the first female mayor. Lucy was quite the busy mayor, interviewing with famous television journalists, accepting stimulus money, and serving as a parade marshall. Lucy even placed three times in the magazine, *Cincinnati CityBeat*'s, category of "Best Elected Official." Apparently, she even considered running for president!

After Lucy, a pit bull named Brynneth Pawltro took over the candidacy when she won the most "votes" with $3,367. For the first time ever, the historical society declared the first and second runners-up, Bourbon and Lady Stone, as Rabbit Hash ambassadors. If the mayor is ever unavailable for an important event, one of these fine dogs can fill in.

The 2020 election had the people of Rabbit Hash holding their breath. No, not to see who the new president would be. They were waiting to see if Wilbur Beast, the French Bulldog, would become the next mayor. Apparently, he won by the largest amount ever, collecting 13,143 of the 22,985 votes. That was a record-breaking amount of money raised for the historical society! Wilbur ran on the platform, "Give me liberty or give me...milkbones." His owner said he has transitioned into the role of mayor easily. "He's done a lot of interviews locally, he's had a lot of pets, a lot of belly scratches, and a lot of ear rubs," she says.

It turns out that any animal can run for mayor. The official rule states that a candidate just needs to be able to chase a rabbit from their residence to the center of Rabbit Hash in one hour's time. Smokey the Rooster and Higgins the donkey were also write-ins on the ballot, so the next mayor of Rabbit Hash may look a little different. This town seems to not take itself too seriously, and knows how to have a good time!

A Well Traveled Dog

This is a story about good-natured people who went out of their way to help an animal. It starts off with a young man named Adam. Adam lived in Pennsylvania and took his two dogs out for their daily walk. He didn't expect to see a loose dog on his walking route and was even more surprised when the dog followed him home.

A large brown coonhound, with a collar, but no nametag was apparently lost and seemed to be asking Adam for help. Luckily, Adam was a dog lover so he took action to see if he could find the lost pet's owners. He probably thought he belonged to somebody nearby.

Adam took the brown dog to the local veterinarian who scanned him for a microchip. Fortunately, the dog did have a microchip with accurate information. But the vet and Adam were shocked! The chip said that this dog's name was Jake and he lived in Phoenix, Arizona, over 2,000 miles away!

The vet asked a local dog rescue agency to step in and help the stray dog. The agency's president, Renae Metz, called Jake's owners who couldn't believe it. Jake had been missing for over a year and a half when he had disappeared from their yard. They had never expected to see him again. They were overjoyed...but they had a problem. The couple had a brand new baby at home and there was no way they could make the 4,000-mile round trip to get Jake.

This is where a bunch of kind strangers stepped up to help. When Jake's owners asked Renae if the rescue had any way to help, she accepted the challenge and got to work. Her sister had a job as a transport coordinator, so this was her jam. She used her contacts and social media to coordinate a safe network of drivers for Jake's trip home. Five days after Jake was found on the streets of Pennsylvania, he started his journey back to his family in Arizona.

Jake wore a t-shirt that said "Arizona or bust". Along the journey, he picked up a new signature for his shirt with every person that helped him along the way. Leaving Pennsylvania, Jake would travel through 7 other states, 30 stops along the way, 20 drivers, and three overnight stops, before reaching Arizona and being reunited with his family. Jake met a lot of new people and gained many new friends along the way. He always greeted everyone with a smile and a puppy kiss as if to thank them for their help.

Jake and his owner were thrilled to be reunited. Jake got to go home and meet the newest member of the family. Thanks to the kindness of strangers, Jake was able to go back to the family that loved him and live the rest of his happy life.

The Guide Horse

Janet and Don Burleson were visiting New York City when they were struck with a flash of insight. Janet had been a horse trainer for 30 years, and she watched in awe as the horses they rode on a Central Park trail ride seemed to be able to read the traffic and know when to cross the street. Janet remembered watching a blind rider whose horse was able to navigate a series of obstacles keeping the rider totally safe. She got home and experimented with her own miniature horse, Twinkie. The idea for using miniature horses as guide horses for the blind was born!

Guide horses offer an interesting alternative to guide dogs. Obviously, a guide horse won't work for every setting. They need to be able to live outside when they are off duty. Their larger size might not work as well in large city settings. But they offer some unique benefits. To a person concerned about the shorter lifespan of their guide dog, a guide horse has a much longer life expectancy. It's also a great alternative for a person with dog allergies.

The Burlesons began training Twinkie as an experiment. She was small enough that she could ride around in their minivan. They found her willing and easy to train and navigate different situations. There were a few problems. The first time she went inside the grocery store she grabbed a Snickers bar off the shelf!

Dan Shaw had suffered from declining vision for nearly 30 years. He knew he would need the help of a service animal or some kind of support. He didn't want to get a dog, as he had recently lost his family dog and found it such a heartbreaking event. He knew it would be even more devastating to lose a dog that was his partner in sight. When he heard about the concept of a seeing-eye horse, Dan was immediately interested. He got in contact with the Burlesons and signed up to be the first recipient of a seeing-eye horse.

The Burlesons selected a miniature horse named Cuddles to be Dan's partner. She went into rigorous training before she and Dan met for the first time. When she was ready, Dan flew to meet her. They worked together for over a month, navigating crowded stores and even an airport! When they were ready, Cuddles went home with Dan, where he had a barn and a pasture ready for her.

With Cuddles by his side, Dan is able to navigate easily through his daily life in his small town. Cuddles is trained to do everything a guide dog would do. She assists Dan with walking through town, alerts him to step up or down, and will even stop moving forward if she senses danger ahead. Dan has to be ready to stop and chat frequently. Everyone is curious and has questions about this cute little guide horse! Luckily, Dan and Cuddles are great ambassadors and are willing to share their story. Dan feels incredibly lucky to have been paired with Cuddles. Not only has she allowed him to live a more independent life, but they also share a special bond. "We are one now. We are a good team," he says.

The miniature horses selected for training must have a trainable, easy-going personality. The horses that are the best fit for the program usually weigh between 55-100 pounds. Much bigger than that and it becomes difficult to navigate them through certain situations. The training program takes about 8 months. They are trained to lead and to respond to voice commands. They are also potty-trained! They learn to go to the door and tap a hoof to alert their owner that they need to go outside. Speaking of hooves, these little guys also wear tiny sneakers to prevent them from slipping. Some blind people think the horses' hooves are a benefit over dogs' feet because you can hear the clip-clop on the ground, which makes them more aware of their surroundings.

Guide horses are recognized as service animals, meaning they would be allowed to go in stores, restaurants, and anywhere a guide dog could go. Dan says that he has never been somewhere that didn't allow Cuddles. While it may be a while before guide horses are as common as guide dogs, this is a neat and clever alternative for those who need one. The Burleson's goal is to create a safe, cost-effective alternative for mobility to help those who are vision impaired. And who doesn't love to see a cute miniature horse walking down the sidewalk helping to make someone's dream of independence come true?

Pizza...and a Dog?

When you place an order for a pizza, this is probably what you expect to get...hot crispy crust, tangy tomato sauce, gooey cheese, and plenty of your favorite toppings. It will most likely come in a square, cardboard box. But just as you reach down to open the box and take that first delicious bite, you notice something. There is a flier attached to the box. You look closer and see a happy, smiling face with his tongue hanging out of his mouth, ears standing at attention. The flyer reads, "My name is Pickles and I'm 2. I live at Niagara SPCA. I'd like to live with you."

This might be the type of scenario you'd find yourself in if you were to order a pizza from Just Pizza & Wing Co. in Amherst, New York. The owner of the pizza shop is Mary Alloy, a long-time dog lover. She began working with the Niagara Society for the Prevention of Cruelty to Animals (SPCA), donating her time and occasionally her pizzas to help with local adoption events. While they were scheming ways to help more dogs get adopted, one of the SPCA event coordinators had an idea. Why not put pictures of the adoptable dogs looking for homes on the pizza boxes?

Mary loved the idea. In fact, she even cried with happiness at being able to help animals in need. That's who Mary is. She likes to give back to her community. Her pizza shop is filled with little boxes available for people to leave donations for local charities. It was a no-brainer for her to attach flyers to her pizza boxes.

The community loved it. The people loved seeing the cute animals attached to their pizza dinners. Mary's Just Pizza shop was selling 600-800 pizzas per week. But when the shop started putting fliers on the boxes, orders really picked up. Within just 2 days, they had sold over 500 pizzas. The community was enjoying this. And it seemed to work. Within one day, a cute little 6-month-old puppy named Larry had already been adopted, thanks to his new owners seeing one of the pizza box fliers.

Mary made dog adoption even more appealing by offering a $50 gift certificate to her Just Pizza shop to anyone who adopted a dog that was featured on one of the fliers. Pizza and dogs...what could be better?!

This popular idea spread to other pizza shops in the country that thought it was a good idea and wanted to help their own local animals get adopted.

Mary's work continued with the SPCA and other community charities. She kept donating pizzas for events and volunteering her time and pizza boxes. About a year and a half later, the SPCA honored Mary in a special way. They permanently named a dog kennel in their facility in her honor. The kennel chosen was located at B-7. Mary's birthday is July 7th or 7/7. At the dedication ceremony, a sign read "B7 In Honor of Mary Alloy, a true friend of the SPCA."

Here's where the story gets even more special. At the dedication ceremony, Mary visited the kennel that had been named for her. Inside she met the kennel's resident, a German Shepherd named Caspian. The dog charmed Mary right away. So much so that Mary's son called his sister and adoption arrangements were soon underway. Caspian was renamed Rocky and has a wonderful new life.

Mary's story is proof that even little acts of kindness can go a long way toward helping. Putting fliers on pizza boxes didn't cost Mary any money or even much time, but it sure did help many dogs find new lives full of joy and family!

Blizzard Rescue

Norman and Eve Fertig ran an animal sanctuary on their property in upstate New York. For years the couple had cared for and rehabilitated animals that needed a little extra help. It was their passion and something that they felt they were called to do.

One of their animals was a giant dog that was part wolf, part German Shepherd. They had rescued the pup when she was only 2 weeks old and in desperate need of care. Shana, as the couple named the pup, ended up staying with them as their pet. She also ended up returning the life-saving favor seven years after her initial rescue.

One late afternoon in October, the couple left their house and went a quarter mile to the building where they housed the sick and injured animals. This was their daily routine. In the late afternoon and early evening, the couple would spend several hours feeding, cleaning, medicating, and caring for all of the animals at their sanctuary. On this particular day, some of the occupants included an 18-year-old raven and a crow that had been shot. The couple went through their routine tasks. Everything seemed normal until the electricity in the barn went out.

When Eve and Norman had left their house to go to the sanctuary it had been a chilly but clear October afternoon. What they found when they went outside a few hours later was that a dark, dangerous, and unexpected blizzard had rolled in. Snow swirled around and the air was bitterly cold. The couple started the walk back to the house, seeking warmth desperately. Just as the couple was nearing their house, a massive tree fell, blocking their path. They lived in a heavily wooded area. With the snow falling rapidly, and the night pitch black, they knew that if they went off the trail, they would risk getting lost. They began to try to remove tree branches and limbs, hoping they could perhaps find a way over or through the enormous tree. But Eve and Norman weren't as spry as they once were. They were both 81 years old. They had not dressed to be out in a blizzard and now they were trapped and feeling the pressure. With each passing minute, the situation was becoming more desperate.

That was when help showed up in the form of a 160-pound part wolf, part German Shepherd. Shana usually went to the sanctuary with her owners and then adventured on her own. When she couldn't find her owners, she went looking for them. Shana took charge of the situation immediately. She began to bark, scurry and dig at the base of the tree. She continued this for hours, and it soon became apparent to Eve and Norman that she was digging them a tunnel. They tried to help, too, but Shana did most of the work, actually clearing and digging a tunnel under the tree to the house. When she was done with her mission, she came back. Eve only weighed 86 pounds, almost half of what Shana weighed. Shana seemed to want Eve to hang onto her back, while Norman leaned on her side and Shana pulled them through the tunnel to safety.

Unfortunately, the danger wasn't over when they reached the house. With no electricity, there was no heat and the couple was still really cold. Shana came to the rescue here, too. She laid on top of the couple as they all huddled together for warmth for the rest of the night. The next morning, rescue crews arrived and began to help remove the giant tree and restore power to the house. The rescue workers were amazed by this furry rescue story and to see the life-saving tunnel that Shana had dug.

The next week Shana was awarded The Citizens For Humane Animal Treatment's Hero Award for bravery. That's an honor that is normally given to humans. But in this case, it seemed fitting to give the award to an animal who was so dedicated to helping her people. Her owners are very grateful and proud of Shana. They hung the award in their living room as a constant reminder of their loyal friend.

Nurse Rescues a Patient's Dog

Jennifer Smith is the type of caring, kind nurse who goes above and beyond for her patients. She recently had the opportunity to show just how much she cares for not only a patient but his pet as well.

John Burley quickly became one of Jennifer's favorite patients when he was admitted to her wing of the nursing and care center where she worked. John was recovering from pneumonia and lung problems and had to be admitted to the center so he could receive supervised medical attention. Before he was in the medical center, John had his own apartment. Most of his family lived far away. John was mostly alone except for the love and friendship of his dog, Boomer. The two had been together for twelve wonderful years.

Because John had no family or close friends nearby, it was becoming increasingly difficult to find anyone to look after Boomer. Unfortunately, the town took matters into its own hands.

When Jennifer arrived at work early one morning she immediately received a phone call with a frantic John on the other end, "Boomer's in the pound! Boomer's in the pound!" he exclaimed.

Jennifer had heard a lot about Boomer from John during their time together. John loved showing photos of Boomer and telling stories about him. It made Jennifer worried and sad to think that John's best friend was in the pound. So she took matters into her own hands and tried to find him. The city they live in has many animal shelters and she didn't know which one had Boomer. It was also Christmas and she worried that Boomer might have already been adopted out to another family. She called around until she found a dog that fit his description. When she told John, he begged her, "Will you take care of Boomer?" Jennifer told him that she would and set off to get him.

After rescuing Boomer, Jennifer took him to the vet and shopping for food, toys, and even doggy sweaters! She wanted to make sure John's little friend was well cared for while he was recovering. Jennifer had a dog of her own so she knew how important these relationships were. She wanted John to be able to focus on getting himself better and know that Boomer was in good hands. This would be one less worry for him.

It turns out Boomer was good for a lot of people. After Jennifer rescued him and brought him to her house to live, she was able to bring him to work to see John. It really lifted John's spirits. He loved riding around in his wheelchair with Boomer on his lap. Boomer lifted the hearts of all of the other patients at the hospital, too. The little 19-pound terrier mix was full of tail wags and kisses for everyone.

"I can see why John loves his dog so much," Jennifer said, "Boomer is fantastic. I walk through the halls with him in the wings and all the residents that are in the hallway, they instantly smile. I let each of them pet Boomer."

Pet therapy has been used for many years. Interactions with therapy animals by hospital patients have been known to lower blood pressure, reduce stress, promote healing and simply bring happiness. What's not to love about soft fur and wagging tails?

While John was focusing on healing, Jennifer made sure Boomer got everything he needed. A dog this special deserved the best possible care while his owner was sick. And he was lucky to find that from an extremely special nurse.

Dog Makes Family Whole Again After Saving Them From a Tornado

Dogs make a family feel complete. They share their love and affection, give us protection, and lots of laughs. Many people that have dogs consider them an important part of the family.

The Johnson family certainly considered their dog, Bella, part of their family. The tan and white mini Australian Shepherd was a big part of their lives. She lived in the house, played with the children, and made everyone happy. So when she was missing, the family was desperate to find her. The story of how they got separated is a crazy story...and the Johnson family may owe Bella their lives.

Spring storms were moving through the area when Eric and his wife, Faith, went to bed that night. Storms like this were common in Tennessee this time of year. When Eric heard Bella come into the room, whining at 1:30 am, he woke up. She continued to whine, and act anxious, crawling under the bed and raising a ruckus. Eric remembered the storms and decided to check the weather. It was looking bad to the west of where they were, with heavy storms heading in their direction. Eric and Faith stayed up and stayed alert, watching the news, ready if they needed to take action.

Suddenly, the storm looked like it was changing direction and moving right toward their neighborhood. They grabbed their two young children, wrapped them in blankets, and put them in the bathtub. Faith crouched down with them. Eric was looking for Bella, and their other dog, Scooter, but both had disappeared. It all happened so fast. Before Eric could find the dogs, or even make it back to his family, the tornado was upon them. It ripped the house apart, tossing Eric into the yard amongst the wreckage.

As soon as it happened, it was over. Eric got up and realized he was in the yard. All he could see was darkness around him and hear the cries of neighbors needing help. Eric had a large wound on the back of his head. But there was only one thing on his mind. He had to find his family.

The debris was extensive. The bathtub where Faith and the kids had been was now sitting in the yard, cracked in half, but everyone was still alive. Faith had clung desperately to the children to keep them safe. She had two broken ribs and a fractured sternum. When she asked the doctor how that was possible, he said it was likely from holding on so tightly to the kids.

The humans in the family were ok, but what about their pets? Sadly, their dog, Scooter, didn't survive. And they couldn't find Bella. As the tornado clean-up began, they watched for any sign of her. Then friends started telling the family that they were seeing a dog that looked just like Bella around town. With her crystal blue eyes, she was especially recognizable. She was scared and didn't seem to want anyone to get close to her. She was still distressed by the whole experience. And who could blame her? Being in a tornado is terrifying for anyone!

For months, the family missed their beloved dog, only getting the occasional sign of her when friends around town would spot her. By the time they would get there, Bella would be gone. They tried leaving clothes with their scent to help her find her way home, but none of it seemed to work.

A friend from their church was a successful dog tracker. She helped by setting up cameras in the areas where Bella had been spotted. Piecing together the clues from the video footage, they were able to figure out Bella's hiding spot. The tracker lured Bella with a cheeseburger and was able to get her trapped in an alley. But Bella was still nervous and didn't want to be caught. Luckily, Eric was on his way. He knew if he could just talk to her everything would be ok. Sure enough, as soon as Bella saw Eric's familiar face, she knew everything was alright. She ran up to him and the two had a wonderful, tearful reunion. After four long months, Bella was going home!

After a quick trip to the vet to make sure Bella was healthy, she was reunited with her whole family. They were so grateful to see her. They lost their house and one dog in the tornado, but having Bella back with them made them feel like they could finally move forward. Thanks to Bella's persistence on that scary night, the family had been able to stay safe during that terrible storm. They could keep her safe and give her plenty of love now that she was back where she belonged.

P-22

People flock to Hollywood every year in the hopes of making it big. They move to the big city and dream of being famous. Los Angeles became famous for its movie and film industry and the town rapidly grew. With the famous Hollywood sign looming in the background, urban sprawl overtook the city as it pushed further and further into the California wilderness.

It turns out that people aren't the only ones moving into Tinseltown. One particularly motivated cat also took the trek into the city. This cat was a little different from most cats you would expect to find living in a large city. That's because this cat is a mountain lion!

That's right. In the heart of L.A. in the area surrounding the iconic Hollywood sign, a mountain lion, named P-22 set up his home. And instead of being afraid, the people of Los Angeles embraced the wild animal, changing laws for his protection and giving him plenty of respect.

So how did a mountain lion decide to move to L.A.? Good question! Fifty miles outside of the city is the Santa Monica mountain range, where P-22 was born in 2010 and lived amongst 100 other mountain lions. He eventually set off on a Hollywood-type adventure where he crossed two major Los Angeles freeways without being seen and eventually settled in the 4000-acre Griffith Park, right in the heart of Los Angeles.

How did P-22 get his name? As a mountain lion born in the Santa Monica mountain range, he was part of a group of large cats being studied by National Parks Service biologists. The P stands for puma and the 22 for the number he was in the recordings. Biologists already had him in their system before he went on his epic journey.

In 2012, Gerry Hans, the president of the Friends of Griffith Park, was doing a camera survey to capture all the different wildlife that were making the park their home. Imagine his surprise when they realized that a mountain lion had been captured in the videos! Gerry wasn't sure how the public was going to react to this news. Mountain lions are fierce creatures. They are wild animals and can be unpredictable.

At first, people were nervous, and rightfully so! But soon, they began to realize that they could co-exist with this wild creature. He was rarely ever seen, keeping to himself and hunting at night. His area that he roams is only about 8 square miles, much smaller than most male mountain lions who cover a range of about 150 square miles. And yet, even with a tracking collar to help find him, researchers hardly ever saw him.

Instead, P-22 chooses to live a quiet existence, never showing off for the camera, despite being the most famous cougar in the world, living in the land of movie stars. And the people of L.A. have embraced this. He has had a few close encounters. He once got sick from eating an animal that had been killed with rat poison.

The public was outraged and insisted a law be passed preventing the sale of all dangerous rodenticides.

When P-22 jumped the fence to the L.A. Zoo and killed a sleeping koala, the public didn't blame him for acting like a wild cat. Instead, the zoo decided to change its policy and began to lock up the zoo animals overnight for their safety. In most other parts of the country, this type of behavior might have led to the mountain lion being destroyed or relocated. But in Los Angeles, P-22 is famous and people are recognizing the need to preserve wildlife.

P-22 has become the "poster puma" for the need for a wildlife bridge crossing. In the spring of 2022, the Wallis Annenberg Wildlife Crossing was established as a way to connect the northern Santa Monica Mountain Range with the Simi Hills in southern California. This land bridge goes over the top of L.A. freeways, giving animals a safe passage to expand into new territories.

P-22 continues to make Griffith Park his home. With no other male mountain lions around to threaten him, scientists hope he will live longer than the average life expectancy of a mountain lion, which is 12 years. To the people of L.A., he's the ultimate cool cat who moved to Hollywood and made it big!

A Dog Survives Both a Tsunami AND 3 Weeks at Sea

Natural disasters are catastrophic events that originate from problems that occur naturally on the earth. Some examples are tornadoes, hurricanes, earthquakes, and blizzards. They often cause damage to property, disrupt everyday routines, and can cause injuries and even deaths. We often think about the impact that natural disasters have on humans. But what about the animals?

It was the biggest and most powerful earthquake ever in Japan. It was actually the fourth most powerful known earthquake ever. It caused widespread devastation and tragedy when it unleashed a monster tsunami in 2011. More than 20,000 people died in this horrible tragedy.

The tsunami washed away thousands of homes. One Japanese coast guard helicopter was making patrols out over the ocean looking for survivors. It was three weeks after the tsunami had struck. Few survivors were being found at this point. It was a grim and depressing job.

The pilots (and the entire country) really needed a piece of good news. And they were about to get it.

"Is that? It's a dog!" The rescuers couldn't believe it. They were out over the ocean more than a mile away from shore. Wreckage was still floating everywhere.

As they flew over the remains of a house, a dog ran out from under the roof to look at them. As they got closer, it got scared and ran back under the wreckage.

They lowered a rescuer to try to talk the dog over so they could pull it up. But this dog, even though it hadn't seen anyone in weeks, wasn't ready to trust them just yet. The helicopter started to run low on fuel so they went back to shore. They notified their colleagues at the coast guard office and a rescue boat was sent out.

The rescuer had to kick a hole in the roof to get in and find the little guy. It didn't take much coaxing before they were able to get the poor frightened pup aboard. The dog realized pretty quickly that they were there to help and she was grateful! She enjoyed getting toweled off and some food in her belly. She had lost a lot of weight but was otherwise in pretty good health.

The coast guard wondered if the dog's owner may have been swept out to sea. The dog was wearing a collar but there was no tag with a name or phone number so they had no idea who she belonged to.

Pictures of the cute brown and white mutt were soon in every newspaper and on every TV station. The owner saw her (along with everyone else in the country) and got through to the coast guard. The woman told them that the dog's name was Ban. Ban was two years old, still practically a puppy. As soon as Ban's owner walked into the room to be reunited with her, Ban jumped up and went crazy with excitement. It was obvious that the dog recognized her. Ban's owner had not expected to see her dog again. She said that she would never ever let go of her.

Three weeks is a long time to survive without food or water. Ban must have gotten lucky and had rainwater to drink every now and then during her three-week ordeal. Did she find fish to eat? Ban was pretty quiet about how she was able to survive that long floating on a house in the ocean. So we'll never really know how she was able to pull off such an unlikely survival. But one thing we know for sure...that's one brave and tough little dog!

The Biscuit

With the Great Depression and World War I happening within a few years of each other, the American people during the 1930s were needing something positive. They needed something to root for after the tough grind of the last 10 years. They didn't know it at the time, but that thing was coming. And it was something that every American could get behind and cheer for...an underdog with the will and heart to win.

That underdog was actually a horse, a racehorse, who would win the hearts of the American people. His story is a bit unconventional, but that's what made it special. He wasn't a big flashy horse that would make you think, "Now, that horse there is a winner!" It was quite the opposite, actually.

Seabiscuit was named after his father. His father was called Hard Tack, which is the name given to a dense biscuit or cracker often used in long journeys over the sea because they lasted a long time. Thus his son was given the name, Seabiscuit.

Seabiscuit wasn't remarkable as a young horse. He was small for a racehorse and had knobby knees that didn't usually lend themselves to speed. Most of all, he seemed to be incredibly lazy, usually taking long naps in his stall, broken up only by his desire to eat. In his early races, it seemed that going out on the racetrack was more of an interruption of naptime and snacktime for Seabiscuit.

He wasn't very fast either. He had a demanding schedule of races for his original owners but pulled off very few wins. He was eventually sold to Charles Howard, who would hire trainer, Tom Smith, for the horse.

Tom had some unconventional training methods that seemed to work for Seabiscuit. Suddenly, the sleepy horse was looking like he wanted to run! Tom and Charles hired a new jockey for Seabiscuit. Red Pollard wasn't a famous jockey, but he and Seabiscuit seemed to have a good understanding. Suddenly, the little horse started winning races and catching the public's attention.

With several big wins under their belt, the team of Charles, Tom, Red, and Seabiscuit decided to try the prestigious race known as "The Hundred Grander". The winner of the Santa Anita Handicap in California would be awarded $125,000! In the practice race leading up to the big event, Seabiscuit was an easy winner. But on the day of the big event, he came in second. What happened? It turns out that the jockey, Red, had been hiding a problem from everyone else. He was blind in one eye. It hadn't affected him until a horse was able to sneak up on him and pass Seabiscuit. Luckily, the public didn't care. They already loved the plucky little racehorse with his unconventional connections.

As Seabiscuit accumulated more wins, his owner and trainer decided to send him back to the east coast to take part in the biggest races around. "The Biscuit" would win 11 of his 15 races that year and be the leading money winner of all horses. Unfortunately, Red Pollard would get injured by another horse and the team had to find a replacement jockey. A friend of Red's would step in and go on to win plenty more races with Seabiscuit, while Red recovered.

During this time, there was another horse that had the attention of the media. War Admiral was a big, fast horse with powerful connections. The public wanted to see a match race of the two best horses, War Admiral and Seabiscuit.

Called the "Match of the Century", the media hailed War Admiral as the clear favorite. He was large and had early speed, something that would be difficult for a smaller horse like Seabiscuit. But Seabiscuit's trainer was ready, keeping the little horse sharp and focused. On the day of the race, Seabiscuit leaped forward and was the clear leader. He only slowed for a few seconds towards the close of the race. Red Pollard had told the jockey riding him a little trick. He slowed Seabiscuit, until the other horse was almost catching up, then let Seabiscuit surge forward to win the race. This little move seemed to help the very competitive Seabiscuit stay motivated and ready for the win.

Fans were even more smitten with Seabiscuit after he won the match race. He was voted American Horse of the Year and was the number one newsmaker across the country.

Then, tragedy would strike. In two separate incidents, both Red and Seabiscuit were injured. Both were considered unlikely to ever race again. But Red had other plans. He worked hard, rehabbing his broken leg and even making a splint to stabilize it. Seabiscuit also made a slow but steady recovery. Before long, Red was galloping Seabiscuit on the track. They convinced his owner that they were ready to race again.

Only one big race still eluded Seabiscuit. He'd come in second place twice in "The Hundred Grander" but they wanted that win. In a heroic effort, showing the clear trust and partnership of the two injured racers, both jockey and horse made an incredible comeback and won the only race they had yet to conquer.

Seabiscuit's well-earned retirement was announced the next spring. He made a lasting impression on the public with over 50,000 people visiting the farm where he retired. Everyone wanted to meet this little unconventional horse who showed so much heart on and off the racetrack. The entire team involved with Seabiscuit's story were considered underdogs and the hard-working American people loved having a team like this to root for. Seabiscuit is still remembered as being one of the best racehorses of this century.

The Smallest Building Ever Designed By a Famous Architect

Do you know what an architect does? An architect designs homes and buildings. They put together the plans for what materials to use, where to use them and how to put them together. They look at things like the overall size and space in a building and often have to get creative with fitting in all the necessary features. Some architects are very famous for designing incredibly creative buildings. These buildings may all have a similar style or features so you can easily distinguish who the architect was.

Frank Lloyd Wright was one of those architects. He has been recognized as the greatest American architect of all time. He designed houses that fit in well with the nature surrounding them. He created the plans and designed the famous Guggenheim Museum in New York City. In other words, he was a very busy and important guy in his day.

So what does this have to do with animals? In 1956, Frank Lloyd Wright was designing a house for the Berger family. One of their sons, Jim, decided that he had a special request for the designer. So he wrote him a letter.

In the letter, Jim asks if Frank will design a dog house for the family dog, Eddie. Jim was 12 years old and was worried about his dog sleeping outside. Eddie was a black labrador retriever and must have been an important part of the family if Jim took the time to write this letter. Jim gave details about Eddie's size, so Frank would know how big to make the dog house. He included that Eddie was "four years old or 28 in dog years." Jim also made sure to tell Frank that he had recently gotten a paper route so he could afford to pay for the dog house plans.

Frank responded to Jim's letter. He told Jim that designing a dog house for Eddie was an opportunity. But he said that at the time he was just too busy to take on another project. He suggested that Jim send him a reminder letter later.

Jim sent the reminder letter at the time Frank suggested. To his surprise and excitement, several weeks later he received the requested plans for a four-square-foot dog house designed specifically for Eddie. The plans utilized extra wood that remained after the Berger's main house was built so that the dog house would blend in perfectly. Looking back Jim says, "My dog had a lot of class, and a Frank Lloyd Wright doghouse was perfect for him. I was very excited for my dog."

However, Jim didn't get around to building the dog house right away. Later, he ended up joining the army and moving away from home. That year, his younger brother, Eric, and his dad decided to try building the dog house. They built it just as suggested, but Eddie would never sleep in it! Silly dog. The family thinks that by that point he had already chosen a warm cozy spot near their door as his favorite sleeping place. "That was kinda depressing," Jim stated later.

Years later, Jim's mother was cleaning out the house and she didn't think anything of throwing the old unused dog house into the trash heap. No one would miss it. And no one thought anything of it until 2010 when some people who were making a movie about Frank Lloyd Wright heard about the dog house story. The filmmakers contacted Jim to see if it would be possible to make another dog house. By this point, Jim and Eric were grown men and skilled woodworkers. This seemed like a project they would enjoy. So the two brothers rebuilt the dog house of their childhood friend, Eddie. Jim says, "In the letter, I said I wanted something easy to build, but this doghouse was not easy to build. It was very complicated."

Still, the brothers pressed on. During filming, the new dog house was installed in the location of the original, right next to the house. On this day it was raining. The crew and the brothers noticed something interesting about the low-slung roof. It leaked! This was a common problem with some of Frank Lloyd Wright's designs using low-pitch roofs. Even the dog house couldn't escape it!

Eddie's House is the littlest building that the famous architect, Frank Lloyd Wright, ever designed. It is now on display at the largest building he ever designed, the Marin County Civic Center in California. The workers at the center say that the dog house is a big hit. The pet-loving community loves this fun family story. It just goes to show that all people love man's best friend!

Fat Bear Week

Basketball fans have March Madness to celebrate their love of the game and participate in an annual tradition of competition. They use brackets to narrow down who the best basketball team of the year will be. Bear and nature lovers have something similar. They call it Fat Bear Week, picking the fattest, healthiest looking bear to be declared the winner at the end of the season before the bears head into hibernation.

Brown bears living in Katmai National Park in Alaska have a pretty good advantage when it comes to growing and putting on weight throughout the spring and summer. The region has the biggest and healthiest run of sockeye salmon in the whole world. These bears are well-fed, and it's a good thing they are. A fat brown bear is a healthy brown bear!

These bears hibernate every winter, which means that they go to sleep in their den and don't wake up for 5-8 months. Talk about missing their alarm clock! The bears do this to avoid the frigid cold of the Alaskan wilderness. Their bodies are designed to slow down for hibernation. Their body temperature, heart rate, and respiration all drop way down. Their body uses the fat stored during the summer season as energy. A bear can lose up to one-third of its body weight while it is hibernating. It is important for a bear to consume a large number of calories and get good and fat each summer to prepare for the next winter. During the summer, a brown bear can consume 80-90 pounds of food per day! They will eat anything such as berries, fruit, grasses, caribou, beavers, and large amounts of salmon.

The rangers at Katmai National Park are proud of their bears and love to see them get big and plump every summer. They decided to share this story of progress with the rest of the world by hosting Fat Bear Week. Not only is it fun, but it helps to educate the public on the ways brown bears live and survive, along with raising awareness for conservation efforts that affect bears and other animals.

Each fall, a group of brown bears is highlighted. The bears are placed in brackets and people can vote for their favorite bear. Fat Bear Week doesn't necessarily mean that the actual fattest bear will win. The rangers can't exactly go around asking the bears to step onto a scale to be weighed! But people can view before and after pictures of each bear. In May or June, when the bears show up to the Brooks River and begin to fish they are just coming out of hibernation. They are usually very skinny and need to start gaining weight to survive. And they do! By Fat Bear Week in the beginning of October, these bears are plump and roly-poly, a true testament to the good fishing in the area and good ole' mother nature.

On the Katmai National Park website, pictures as well as information and stories about the bears will help voters decide on their favorites. The bracket winners will advance to the next round, narrowing the pool each day so that the most popular bears advance. At the end of Fat Bear Week, a new champion is crowned!

A recent addition to the Fat Bear Week bracket is another form of fun. People can also vote for the Fat Bear Junior. Four chubby cubbies compete against each other and the winner has a chance to enter the senior competition and be judged against the bigger bears.

People have enjoyed voting for their favorite fat bears since the challenge began in 2014. Each year, the contest grows in popularity. People tune in to live "Bear Cam" throughout the year to see how these wild creatures live and interact in the wild. Over 800,000 people voted in the 2021 bracket, the largest year yet. If you want to participate in the Fat Bear Week voting and learn more about brown bears, check out the website explore.org.

Escaped Orangutan!

The movie, Madagascar, tells the story of the crazy adventures of several escaped zoo animals. But zoo animals don't escape regularly, right? And they certainly don't get up to silly antics while they are outside their enclosures. While it's true that most zoo animals stay safely enclosed in their zoo habitats, this is the story of one rascally orangutan and his adventures at the San Diego Zoo.

Ken Allen doesn't sound like the name of an ordinary orangutan, but Ken Allen was not an ordinary orangutan. Before the days of social media and news stories that spread like wildfire, Ken Allen was making a name for himself as the ultimate escape artist.

Ken Allen was born in captivity, meaning his mom was already living in a zoo. When he was very young, his mother wasn't very nice to him and he had to be rescued by two zoo keepers, Ken Willingham and Ben Allen. Now you see how he got his name!

As a young orangutan, Ken Allen was known for taking the bolts off of his cage and exploring the orangutan nursery at night. By morning he would have put himself back in his enclosure and fastened the bolts before any of the zookeepers returned. This was a sign of the mischief to come.

In June of 1985, Ken Allen managed to escape from his exhibit at the San Diego Zoo and walk down a path filled with tourists. He stopped to observe the other animals as if he himself were just a regular zoo customer. His keepers found him and led him back to his enclosure.

After his first escape, zoo personnel extended his enclosure, ramping up security measures by adding a moat and a massive wall. But just a few weeks later, he was able to find his way out again. This time, he was found throwing rocks at another orangutan named Otis! At one point Otis had lived in the same pen as Ken Allen and was known for not being easy to get along with. It seemed as though Ken Allen was teasing Otis that he was still locked up!

A month later Ken Allen found a crowbar that a worker had accidentally left in his enclosure. He gave the crowbar to a pen-mate, Vicki and she was able to pry open a window. Ken Allen was on the loose again!

After this third escape, zoo security was getting desperate to find out how he was able to escape so easily. Ken Allen had learned not to cause any trouble with zookeepers around watching. He could recognize their uniforms, so his keepers started dressing in normal clothes, and acting as zoo visitors in the hopes of catching him in the act. But they couldn't fool Ken Allen!

The zoo hired professional rock climbers to see how he was managing to scale the wall of his enclosure. They added electric wire to the top of the moat wall to prevent him from being able to go any further.

For a while, all of these extra measures seemed to work. But two years later, a clogged water pump caused the moat in his enclosure to dry up. Ken Allen saw his opportunity and ran with it. He literally walked across the moat, climbed the wall, and hoisted himself out of his pen. He was seen walking around taking photos with zoo customers and shaking their hands when a zoo employee spotted him. Workers cleared the area, but Ken made a break for it, heading towards the lion enclosure. Luckily, he was able to be captured before going in with the lions. That probably would have ended badly for Ken Allen!

Trying to distract him from his escape artist tactics, the zoo added more friends into his enclosure. But it turns out that Ken Allen wasn't a good influence on his new friends. A few months after their arrival, Jane and Kumang were found outside of the exhibit, walking around.

The zoo spent $45,000 adding new security to the orangutan pens and the escapes finally stopped. There had been nine escapes total and Ken Allen had become famous. During his later escapes, he was cheered on by tourists as the zookeepers tried to catch him. The zoo even capitalized on their Houdini by printing t-shirts with local news headlines about the escaped primate. Bumper stickers were sold that read *Free Ken Allen*. He had a fan club that called themselves the Orang Gang and printed a newsletter. A local psychiatrist turned songwriter even wrote a song about his escapades. *The Ballad of Ken Allen* became an instant local hit!

With his breakout days behind him, Ken Allen settled down and had good behavior for the next 13 years. When he was 29 years old he was diagnosed with B-cell lymphoma and sadly died. The zoo installed a memorial in his honor. Members of the Orang Gang came and visited him before he passed and even held a candle-lit vigil after his death. It seemed fitting to honor their hairy friend one last time and recount the good ole' days when Ken Allen was evading zoo keepers and causing good fun havoc in the San Diego zoo!

The Long Journey Home

In 1923, the Brazier family took a rambling family road trip from their home in Silverton, Oregon to Wolcott, Indiana. With them for the journey was their beloved pet dog, Bobbie. Bobbie was a bob-tailed Scottish Collie and English Shepherd mix. The dog rode along in the car with his family, stopping at rest areas along the way and enjoying the adventure. They were staying in Wolcott and Frank Brazier decided to go fill the car up with fuel. As usual, Bobbie went along to the gas station. While Frank was in the store, he heard Bobbie yelp. Frank hurried outside to see four of the town's local stray dogs chasing after Bobbie. Frank couldn't catch up to them, but he had little doubt that Bobbie would make it back to where they were staying. Bobbie was usually able to take care of himself and find his way home.

After a few hours, there was still no sign of Bobbie. The Brazier family drove through town honking their horn. Back home, anytime they honked the car horn, Bobbie would show up to go for a ride. But this time it didn't work. The family went to sleep after midnight, sad but hopeful that Bobbie would turn up in the morning.

The next morning, Frank got on the phone and called everyone around town to alert them of the missing dog. He placed pictures in the local newspaper, but no one had seen the family pet. The family remained in Wolcott for another three weeks, postponing the rest of their trip, in order to search for Bobbie. They were heartbroken when he was never found, and knew that they would have to return to Oregon without him. Frank left specific instructions to people in the town that if Bobbie did return, the family would pay for his train ride back to them in Oregon.

The family made it home safely but their hearts were heavy. Fall gave way to a dreary, cold winter. Six months after they had lost Bobbie in Indiana, one of the Brazier daughters, Nova, and her friend were walking through town. Suddenly the girls stopped and stared at a shaggy skinny dog that was walking out of the woods ahead of them. Nova cried out, "Bobbie?!" The little dog shook all over and ran to her. He jumped into her lap and covered her face with kisses, whimpering with joy and relief. Bobbie had miraculously returned home!

The family was sure it was truly Bobby because of three distinct scars. The first was a scar over his eyebrow from when he was kicked by a horse. The second was a scar on his leg when he had been hit (but unharmed) by a passing tractor. And the last identifiable mark was two chipped teeth, thanks to an unfortunate encounter with a gopher. This dog was indeed their Bobbie!

Bobbie was very skinny, wearing an unfamiliar collar, and had extremely sore and bleeding feet. But he was home at last! The condition of his feet led the family to ask the question, "Did Bobbie walk all the way from Indiana?" With his feet rubbed nearly to the bone, it seemed that it was indeed likely that Bobbie had made the 2,800-mile trip on foot. He went home with Nova to recover. Frank said, "Poor Bob was almost all in. For three days he did little but eat and sleep."

As Bobbie was home recovering and enjoying time with his family, his popularity began to rise as his story spread. The local newspaper in Silverton covered the story and it was picked up by newspapers across the nation. He was featured in *Ripley's Believe It or Not* and starred in the movie, *The Call of the West*. As his story spread, tales started trickling in of people who had helped him during his cross-country journey. He would show up in a small town, looking bedraggled, tired, and hungry. He suffered from wounds and exhaustion, but kind, dog-loving strangers would take him in, feed him, doctor his wounds, and give him a safe place to sleep. They all said he seemed grateful but eager to get on with his journey. The Braziers were able to trace most of his journey, finding that he was often seen in towns where they had stopped for the night on their journey back. This led them to believe he was following their scent. Bobbie's journey was over 2,800 miles and he averaged 14 miles a day. He went through plains, deserts, and the Rocky Mountains during the coldest part of the year.

Bobbie became a national hero. He received more fan mail that year than both President Calvin Coolidge and Harry Houdini combined! He was mailed jeweled collars, medals, trinkets, and even the keys to some cities! Bobbie was the guest of honor at a big event in Portland. Over 40,000 people waited in line to meet and pet him. At the end of the event, he was presented with a giant deluxe dog house. Probably the most memorable part of the experience, at least for Bobbie, was when the city of Silverton deemed him exempt from the leash laws, allowing him to roam the streets freely. After all, if he could find his way across the country, he could likely make his way home a few blocks away.

When Bobbie died several years later, the mayor of Portland gave his eulogy. Famous canine movie star Rin Tin Tin laid a wreath at his grave. His grave had the deluxe dog house placed near it and for a while, it was a popular tourist attraction. But more than fame and notoriety, Bobbie's journey brought him back to the love and devotion of his family. Frank Brazier said, "His dog sense and his love for us led him over three thousand miles, across river and prairie, through towns and wilderness, straight to his own folks." Dogs are truly remarkable and faithful creatures and humans are lucky to have them for companions.

A Penguin's New Shoes

Luca is an African penguin who lives in the San Diego Zoo. He is four years old, which means he is in the prime of his life to be doing everything a penguin should be doing: climbing rocks, swimming, and socializing with other penguins.

There is just one problem. Luca suffers from a condition called bumblefoot. This is a condition that affects some birds and small rodents. Bacterial infections in the foot cause sores and swelling, making it painful to walk and get around. You can see where this would be a problem for a social animal such as a penguin. If the sores are left untreated, the bacteria can actually spread to the inside of the body causing internal problems and even death. Luckily, Luca has a great care team at the zoo. But while his bumblefoot could be managed, it still didn't prevent his feet from hurting and making it hard for him to be active.

African penguins are actually on the endangered species list. Conservationists and workers at the zoo know that it is important to protect them. Plus, the people at the zoo just like Luca and want to make sure he can lead a happy life. They decided to see what options were available to help Luca with his feet.

The company Thera-Paw, designs special boots for animals to help them be more comfortable and active. This includes protective wear that prevents slipping,

wraps that help with arthritis pain, and support for sore paws. The people at Thera-Paw were happy to design small penguin boots for Luca's webbed feet. The boots were made of neoprene and rubber, to give him plenty of cushion and prevent rubbing. They are put on using velcro straps so they are easy to take off to make sure his feet are staying clean and treat any sores. The boots are black, just like Luca's feet. They didn't want his boots to make him stand out too much. Would other penguins make fun of him?

To create the boots, specialists made Luca walk over a platform of sand. They were then able to use the prints left in the sand as a mold to make boots that were designed just for Luca.

It didn't take long for Luca to get used to life with his new boots. While the penguin had once been shy and lonely, not able to actively participate in the penguin colony, he is now thriving. Climbing over rocks, meeting other penguins, making a nest, and swimming are all activities that occupy Luca's days now.

Thanks to some special shoes and some good caretakers, this penguin can go on to live a full and happy life, which is what we want for all animals, but especially those that are considered endangered. Plus a penguin wearing shoes is just cute to think about!

YOUR REVIEW

What if I told you that just one minute out of your life could bring joy and jubilation to everyone working at a kids book company?

What am I yapping about? I'm talking about leaving this book a review.

I promise you, we take them **VERY seriously**. Don't believe me?

Each time right after someone just like you leaves this book a review, a little siren goes off right here in our office. And when it does we all pump our fists with pure happiness.

A disco ball pops out of the ceiling, flashing lights come on...it's party time!

Roger, our marketing guy, always and I mean always, starts flossing like a crazy person and keeps it up for awhile. He's pretty good at it. (It's a silly dance he does, not cleaning his teeth)

Sarah, our office manager, runs outside and gives everyone up and down the street high fives. She's always out of breath when she comes back but it's worth it!

Our editors work up in the loft and when they hear the review siren, they all jump into the swirly slide and ride down into a giant pit of marshmallows where they roll around and make marshmallow angels. (It's a little weird, but tons of fun)

So reviews are a pretty big deal for us.

It means a lot and helps others just like you who also might enjoy this book, find it too.

You're the best!
From all of us goofballs at Big Dreams Kids Books

178

Made in the USA
Middletown, DE
29 November 2022

16460844R00099